CW00550516

CLUB CLASS
IN
ASIA PACIFIC
The Insiders' Guide to Private Members' Clubs

Editor
VALERIE HO

Editorial Director
TIMOTHY AUGER

Production Manager
SIN KAM CHEONG

Art Director
TAN SEOK LUI

Designed and produced by
EDITIONS DIDIER MILLET
121 Telok Ayer Street #03-01
Singapore 068590
www.edmbooks.com

Text © STEPHEN SIMMONS

Colour separated by
UNITED GRAPHIC, SINGAPORE

Printed by
MAINLAND PRESS, SINGAPORE

ISBN: 978-981-4217-43-9

*Penang Sports Club, The British Club, The Helena May Club
(cover, left to right); Stained glass windows, United Service Club
(previous page); Penang Club (pages 2–3); galleried landing, The
Christchurch Club (pages 4–5); poolside, Penang Club (page 6);
ante room, The Christchurch Club (page 8)*

CLUB CLASS
IN
ASIA PACIFIC

The Insiders' Guide to Private Members' Clubs

S.G. SIMMONS

Stephen Simmons

Editions Didier Millet

CONTENTS

Foreword

*P*rivate members' clubs in the Asia-Pacific region could have few more eloquent or convincing champions than Stephen Simmons. Shunning the ephemeral attractions of modern, businessmen's hotels, he delights in the idiosyncrasies and histories of 28 of the region's clubs. Their comfortable individuality becomes his antidote to the luxuriance and 'sterility' of 'globally homogeneous' hotels. While the uncovering of an extraordinary web of reciprocal links should be sufficient enticement to the clubs' members, this book will be fascinating to anyone with an interest in the region or who would simply enjoy a peep behind the doors of some secluded and rarefied places.

That there is an abundance of verandahs with great views, swimming pools, some impressive wine cellars and restaurants serving superb food may not be so surprising, but the clubs individually and variously also comprise or possess: memberships of between 400 and 10,000, including one with 71 nationalities and one boasting 84 reciprocal links; founders as diverse as ladies, the military, 'bohemia', journalists, sailors, race-goers and merchants; means of access as unusual as a sampan, a tunnel, or a network of jungle pathways; facilities which number a racecourse, a golf course, 7 cricket wickets, a 400-metre seafront, a ten-pin bowling alley, a stage, fireplaces and even a bar displaying 47 malt whiskies; an Egyptian skull, the head of a 371-lb swordfish, some magnificent art and medal collections and a library of 25,000 books; mentions in the works of Rudyard Kipling and John le Carré; a club whose current membership includes British royalty and one which used to be regularly graced by a royal saxophonist; and, as a fitting testament to their durability, one which has even survived an earthquake.

Satisfying the primary aim to provide an entertaining compendium, *Club Class* does so with such beautifully observed insights that it could only be the work of someone who has considerable personal experience of both private members' clubs and the region. Elegantly illustrated by many atmospheric photographs, the only disappointment is that it is limited to a somewhat curious roll of 28; but then this is a book about sublime idiosyncrasy.

Nick Shryane
Harrow
London

Preface

A little oddly perhaps, *Club Class in Asia-Pacific* was born in Africa. It was the summer of 2002. A former Hong Kong-based soldier and indeed 'child' of the Far East, I was by then 8 years into a second career working for a Hong Kong-based Investment Bank. Markets were good, new opportunities proliferated and the company was busy going global at a breakneck rate, with offices in dozens of cities around the world. Head offices like to head, whether they need to or not and all of our 'outstations' at one time or another, were the lucky recipients of a morale-raising supervisory visit from senior management. In the early years I was the lucky visited, always grateful for the proffered advice of course. Later I became one of the visitors and was naturally equally generous with my own words of wisdom. Whatever the case, both the airlines and the chain hotels were grateful for our business and they certainly had plenty of it.

The popular myth, generally maintained by those who do not have to do it, says that business travel is all business-class seats, fizz, 5-star hotels, snap decisions on which rest fortunes and brief encounters with dynamic women for whom a glass ceiling is either an optional extra in an interesting boudoir, or merely that metaphorical fly to be swatted on the ascent to the Main Boardroom. Reality, as any 'frequent flyer' will tell you, is, of course, quite different. Reality, almost unfailingly, is a 14-stone body odour problem in the adjacent seat who travels with his socks off and who dribbles, copiously, when asleep. Reality is countless toasts with filthy fire-water, decisions reached only after agonisingly long conference calls and encounters, certainly brief, sometimes passionate too, but generally with hard-faced taxi drivers whose meters mysteriously and regularly fail, usually when it's both raining hard and late in the day. But the reality which eventually

makes the hardened flyer positively ache for the normal human imperfections and foibles of home is the clean, comfortable, easy, efficient, utterly characterless and impersonal concrete business hotel, the cloned and recloned 'accommodation unit' which conceals its geographical or national identity so successfully that the tired guest could be forgiven for believing that he has at last become a citizen of a supra-national state called bizotel.

It was advice time again. By now a rather bored and certainly tiring veteran of countless miles of wholly unromantic business travel, I was in the air again, this time to Johannesburg for a five-week stint. Africa though, was different! Africa was new ground to us and I arrived both excited and curiously bullish, refreshed by the challenges of a new country and of new markets, anticipating a naturally blindingly successful first day at the Exchange, followed by a few celebratory drinks on the verandah of what was not to be, hope springing eternal, a sterile, businessman's box but a quite lovely, Cape Dutch hotel with views out over its own lush and profitable vineyard, suitable reward for such a long period away from home.

It must, of course, have been the air.

Lulled into a false sense of security by both a comfortable flight and a good day in the dealing room, the forlorn hope of a lovely hotel collapsed into the inevitable reality of the brutish exterior of just another hermetically sealed, standard business box, then died, crushed under the weight of an internal confusion of different architectural and cultural styles. Here, Doric columns abounded, Rembrandts were two a penny and muzak was everywhere. This was worse than ever before. This was fusion gone mad and I sought refuge in food and a bottle, only for my head to be sent

Stained glass window, Hong Kong Football Club (page 10); dining room, Naval and Military Club, Melbourne (left) and hall, Hawkes Bay Club (far left)

spinning as a Somali wished me 'bon appetite', in the sushi bar which nestled so very conveniently between the Pizzeria and the Korean restaurant. Control, of a loose but nonetheless very present kind, extended throughout: even the central air-conditioning, set to permafrost, could not be adjusted without the production of a valid medical certificate. The ubiquitous, yet somehow semi detached hotel staff were polite but, in a mildly disquieting, eerily happy way and I began to dread being asked if I too, was 'happy sir?' I half feared the telephone ringing at 2 am only to be asked if I was having a good kip. But worse than all that was the global homogeneity of the hotel… I could have been literally anywhere in the world. My own personal tipping point, at last, had come. I had suddenly tired of business travel and more pertinently of business hotels, and the five weeks I was due to spend in Jo'burg began to stretch out ahead of me like a sentence.

In my room, disconsolate, I picked up Charles Allen's excellent *Tales from the South China Seas*, a charming collection of reminiscences of soldiers, planters and civil servants who had made their lives 'out East'. And as I turned the pages I remembered a chance meeting I'd had in the E&O Hotel in Penang over a dozen years before with the unwilling 'star' of the book, Sjovald Cunyngham-Brown, a man, as it transpired, truly of another time. Then, as I read on, something which he had said to me began to strike an as yet unconscious chord.

This man Cunyngham-Brown had joined the Malayan Civil Service (MCS) ten years before the beginning of WW2 and had quite simply never gone 'Home'. Serving initially as a District Officer in Malacca before a posting to Johore as Deputy Resident,

Entrance, Penang Club (above); The Helena May Club (right); ceiling light in Victoria Room, Royal Automobile Club of Australia (following page)

he volunteered, on the outbreak of war, for service in the Malayan Royal Naval Volunteer Reserve. Surviving two sinkings, he was captured by the Japanese on the island of Sumatra enduring the next three years in a prisoner-of-war camp. Then, in 1945, he headed straight back to his beloved Malaya, remaining there in the MCS throughout the Emergency, ending his career where he had at one time acted as Resident Commissioner: Penang. This was where my wife and I were introduced to him one day, in the lobby of the E&O Hotel. Enthralled, we spent an hour listening to Cunyngham-Brown tell of his 50 years in the Far East. So vivid were his descriptions, articulated in a language so of its time, that rubber estates, gin slings, the P&O Line and the War became almost tangible recollections, even to us. Our plan had been to drive through Malaysia and on to Singapore and we asked him to tell us what we should see of his time as we drove down through the Peninsula. It was the 'ordinary' things which we wanted to see, not the architectural edifices but the quarters, the clubs, the bars and the like which were the stuff of everyday life and with which we, as ordinary people about our own everyday lives, could identify. He was a walking travel guide of course, but of the structures, the buildings which had housed and hosted his early life, it was the old Clubs which Cunyngham-Brown enthused over the most—'gorgeous fun we had then, gorgeous fun' as he thought back to the social life of an era now gone. And then: 'Hated living in hotels—couldn't stand 'em—but my Club reciprocated everywhere—never stayed anywhere else but Clubs from one end of the East to the other'.

At which point in my reverie that earlier struck chord became rather more conscious and as I looked around the comfortable

sterility of my room, I regretted not having taken Cunyngham-Brown's wise words on board years earlier. I had belonged to a Services Club in London for years: why then I wondered, had I never thought of staying in reciprocal Clubs on these long trips away from home rather than succumb, as I had all these years, to the oh-so-easy default mindset of business trip equals business hotel. What a fool I had been to taxi, sheep-like, to the allotted bizotel along with the rest of the sighing crowd. So I picked up the telephone, I called my Club and asked for their reciprocal list of clubs in Jo'burg and I found, The Inanda Club.

The Inanda was located near the new financial district in the opulent northern suburb of Sandton. Founded as a polo club in the late 1800s, the Inanda was a settled, comfortable oasis. The clubhouse was a large, handsome, solidly constructed colonial building with tall ceilings, soft pastel colours and lovely views out over jacaranda and bougainvillea-filled grounds from wide, cool verandahs. A low murmur of camaraderie emanated from the bar, young mothers tended their laughing broods by the pool, tennis partners their bruised knees over a drink on the verandah. I was no longer merely a visitor to Jo'burg: I was, at least temporarily, part of it. My room was not a room but half a small bungalow, not glitzy but clean and spacious. The food in the club was excellent and the service was calm and polite. I was never sold anything: I bought. The grounds, tennis courts and swimming pool were immaculate. As with so many of these members only, well-established clubs, it felt like a cross between a quietly exclusive resort and the private country house of a comfortably off friend. The Inanda was a joy and the sentence had suddenly become rather too short.

Introduction

*I*t has been said that the first thing two Englishmen do when they go and live abroad is form a club, if only to have, as George Orwell thought, some exclusive turf on which to snub each other. The British Club, which grew out of the 17th-century coffee houses and which spread across London, provided in its exported form, the social cohesion of expatriate communities far and wide whether they were planters up-country, 'officials' in the towns or settlers in the Old Commonwealth. The prevalent Victorian, muscular Christianity ethos was the reason behind many opening as sports clubs such as the Hong Kong Football Club or the Penang Swimming Club. Not that all of the Clubs were started by the British of course, but most were modelled on the lines of the British Clubs. Reciprocity itself was simply a system designed to allow for example, a member of the Tanglin Club in Singapore to use, say, the United Services Recreation Club in Hong Kong when that member went to Hong Kong on business or on leave (and vice versa). The Empire was big so it was perfectly possible for this same Tanglin member to find himself in Nairobi or in Cape Town, so reciprocity grew worldwide.

As time passed and society changed, so did the Clubs. It would be unwise to generalise too widely about the flavour now of Clubs in Asia Pacific, just as it would be to generalise about European Clubs: what you find in, say, Oporto, will

The Dunedin Club dinner menu signed by Scott and Shackleton prior to departure for the South Pole (right) and The British Club, Bangkok (facing page)

of course have a different feel to what you find in London. But to help us, we can break them down either nationally or geographically, just a little.

In Australia and in New Zealand, the city Clubs, often being modelled upon London lines have that London or indeed Edinburgh feel and they have changed in a similar fashion to those in the UK: women (generally) no longer barred, IT upgrades, fitness centres and the like, and the ambience is one of urban sophistication. These Clubs stand on their own—London is not necessarily the benchmark anymore, so to say that the Christchurch Club for example, or Brisbane's United Service Club would give any London Club a run for its money is a statement of (what the author sees as) fact in absolute terms, not the drawing of a comparison between the leader and the led.

By contrast, most in South East Asia were formed as gentlemen's sports clubs, Europeans only, with the majority eventually developing into multiracial, family recreation clubs, which still form at least part of the social centre of both expatriate and local life. Wherever they are, South East Asia, New Zealand or Australia, most successful clubs now are full, waiting lists can be long and the membership of most consists of an eclectic mix of different nationalities. Many of the Clubhouses are stunning and if picked up and moved to Surrey would be listed up to the

eaves. Some of the sports facilities are truly excellent. All of the clubs have character. Not all of them have accommodation but even those which do not still have all of the feeding/watering/ recreational facilities which the visiting businessman or family would want, always at lower cost than a hotel and nearly always in a Clubhouse and grounds which are the envy of nearby, newer hotels. Those without accommodation will often have deals with local hotels for cheap(er) rates. What they do all have in common however is membership, to a greater or lesser degree, of this worldwide system of reciprocation. And of course this is the catch for anybody wanting to use one of these Clubs: they are exclusive, not by dint of wads of cash but by dint of belonging to one of their number, somewhere in the world, in the first place. And if you do not belong, then consider joining one and your holiday in Hong Kong or your business trip to Australia, comes with a different and delightful hue.

Great hotels and chic boutique resorts often appear in the travel pages of the Sunday Newspapers: the world wants to travel and the papers show people where and how. Private Clubs however, do not appear because, well, they are exactly that— private. No point in a Sunday running an article on a subject which 95 per cent cannot 'buy'. But the lucky five per cent, the members of this loose confederation of reciprocating Clubs, can

"...they are exclusive, not by dint of wads of cash
but by dint of belonging to one of their number,
somewhere in the world, in the first place."

The Northern Club; The Helena May Club; Taiping New Club;
The Dunedin Club (from left to right)

buy and my aim in writing this guide is to show that five per cent some of the 'best' Clubs I have discovered, from Bangkok to Brisbane. I have visited or revisited each and every one during the course of the last year and also many others which could not quite make the book. As these are private members' Clubs, it has been an enormous privilege for me to have been granted access, particularly to the many to which I had no reciprocal privileges. By so kindly opening their doors to me, they have enabled me to write this guide, the first and only one of its kind, and I am grateful. Reciprocal members are always welcome: hence this book, but the reader should be reminded that reciprocity is a privilege, that the clubs guard their privacy, and that some can be quite unforgiving!

Whilst objectivity has been at the forefront of intent, best, I admit, is a tough word. One man's 'best' is, to misquote appallingly, another man's quite ghastly. So apologies in advance if any of my recommendations appall you (unlikely) or if any omissions outrage you (perhaps more likely).

Do not look upon this book as a Gazetteer: I have not attempted to A–Z every club in Asia Pacific, I have merely chosen my top 28, each one selected because there is something special about it whether it be a fascinating history, views to die for, Olympic sports facilities or simply an outrageously magnetic

No. 199 Taiping, Perak Club.

Perak Club, Taiping

bar. Perhaps most importantly, I have tried to make this guide practical—the clubs must be useable to a visitor on his or her own or with a family, not solely of historical or architectural interest. Nor have I, for reasons of space, listed every allied club at the end of each write-up as some have over 100: I have included a list of the more well known in Asia, the UK, Canada, New Zealand, Australia and parts of Africa. Go to the websites or write to the clubs directly for a full list.

A final word or two of caution. Whilst several Clubs are modernised to a tee, some are not: they don't do luxury, they do comfort and there is a world of difference between the psychology of the two words. Each to his or her own of course, and if your thing is gold taps, bath towels as thick as a shelf of Hello! magazines and hot and cold running waiters, then most of these clubs and certainly this book, are not for you. These are generally (but not always), celebrity-free and polenta-cautious zones. If, however, the mildly idiosyncratic appeals, so too (some) serious views (most of these were built by the British well over a century ago and our forbears pinched a lot of the good real estate) and that comfortable feeling of belonging, often combined with enough pools and tennis courts and the like to keep the most inexhaustible of children happy, then perhaps they are.

HONG KONG

Foreign Correspondents' Club
The Helena May Club
Hong Kong Football Club
Ladies' Recreation Club
Royal Hong Kong Yacht Club
United Services Recreation Club

Foreign Correspondents' Club entrance (above); The Helena May Club (right and previous pages)

I must go down to the Club again for the

Mah Jong call is strong.

I want to throw the dice again, I want to

Pang and Kong.

I must go down to the Club again, the Club

That I can't pass by,

And all I ask is a gin sling to quench

My thirst when I am dry.

I must go down to the Club again, though

It is but half a life,

For a lonely man, 'tis the only way, for a

Man without a wife'.

Anonymous

Foreign Correspondents' Club

The bar

The Foreign Correspondents' Club of Hong Kong is a thriving, wonderfully alive institution, the history and character of which is inextricably intertwined with that of post War Asia. The Club positively hums with life and has, justifiably, a tremendous reputation within the Territory and also throughout the Far East.

The Club was founded, on the hoof so to speak, in Chiang Kai-Shek-controlled Chongqing, China, in 1943 by foreign war reporters. The location of the Club followed the ebb and flow of the war between the Nationalists and the Communists, first to Nanjing, then to Shanghai and then finally to Hong Kong. After several temporary homes, in 1982, Governor Sir Murray Maclehose granted the Club the lease on its premises in the old Ice House at the top of Ice House Street on Hong Kong Island, in one of the few period buildings remaining in Hong Kong.

2 Lower Albert Road
Central
Hong Kong

Tel: +852 2521 1511
Fax: +852 2868 4092
www.fcchk.org
Email: fcc@fcchk.org

The Verandah

Bert's Bar

This vibrant Club, so full of character, is a social, cultural and professional melting pot. If you want to know what is going on politically or socially in Hong Kong then go to the FCC. It is a thrill merely to enter the building knowing that all of the newsworthy events of Asia within the last 50 years have been reported from the newsroom (or from the newsroom of earlier premises in the old Hilton Hotel) from the Vietnam War through Pol Pot's Cambodia to Tiananman Square. The Bar (mentioned in a John Le Carré novel), inevitably, is the place where much of the work gets done and where the business of the professional journalist, i.e. communication, is practised before the formal filing of stories from the newsroom. It is large yet intimate, tall-ceilinged, permanently buzzing and almost impossible to leave. Whilst, naturally enough, it is the journalists who feel their

Food & Beverages
Main Dining Room
Main Bar
Bert's Bar
Verandah
Chinese Restaurant

Sports facilities
Gymnasium
Golf society

Miscellaneous
Library
Workroom
Sauna
Jacuzzi

Accommodation
The Club has corporate deals with several hotels ranging from the YMCA to the Mandarin Oriental. Check the websites for details.

Hemingway moment coming on here, for the rest of us, we need merely be sentient to sense the atmosphere: it is tremendous. Photographs taken by some of the world's greatest photographers decorate the walls and constitute sufficient reason to visit the bar in themselves. Anybody wishing to feel that indefinable but thrilling 'buzz' of Asia cannot help but feel it in the bar of the FCC, particularly on a Friday evening.

A circular staircase displaying some excellent black-and-white photographs of old Hong Kong leads to the Main Dining Room on the first floor. The dining room is smart, serves first rate Asian and Western food and is often the venue for talks from prominent figures from all walks of life. A guest list over the years consisting of Sir Richard Branson, Lee Kuan Yew, Lord (Bill) Deedes, George Soros, Edna Everage, Sir Peter Ustinov and Dave Allen gives an idea of the diversity and calibre of speaker and also of the pull of the FCC. The Verandah area next to the main dining room is less formal, lighter and provides a lovely alternative to the Main Dining Room.

Bert's Bar, named after Bert Okuley, Club member, noteworthy correspondent and fine Jazz pianist, is in the basement. It serves drinks, snacks and features live Jazz three times per week. There is a newly renovated gymnasium, sauna and jacuzzi, a very useful and practical workroom and a library. Accommodation is not available but the Club has a number of excellent corporate deals with local hotels for visiting and reciprocating members. The Club lies five minutes by taxi from Central and Admiralty MTR stations. The website is clear, informative and up-to-date, and contains hyperlinks with reciprocating clubs. All in all, a truly stimulating, wonderful Club.

RECIPROCAL CLUBS

UK
London Press Club
The New Cavendish Club

Thailand
Foreign Correspondents' Club

Singapore
Foreign Correspondents' Club
Hollandse Club
Singapore Cricket Club

Australia
Brisbane Polo Club
The Canberra Club
The Kelvin Club
National Press Club
United Service Club
The Western Australian Club

New Zealand
National Press Club
The Northern Club

The Helena May Club

Dining room

In the early years of the last century, the Crown Colony of Hong Kong was already well set upon the path which would eventually lead it to become the hugely successful port it is today. Trade between east and west was growing at a tremendous rate, serviced by an expanding fleet of cargo ships plying the route from Tilbury Docks via the Suez Canal to Victoria Harbour. Economic success inevitably attracted a growing throng from the UK of those keen to make their fortunes and the influx soon overwhelmed the capacity of the territory's limited number of hotels. Indeed, recently arrived Europeans sleeping rough near the docks became a not uncommon sight. At the same time as this, the Ching Dynasty in China collapsed and the Chinese Republic was proclaimed. There then followed a steady stream of mainlanders moving to Hong Kong, also attracted by the strong

35 Garden Road
Central
Hong Kong

Tel: +852 2522 6766
Fax: +852 2537 5258

www.helenamay.com
Email: info@helenamay.com

Club entrance

Guest room

economy. Lady May, wife of the Governor Sir Henry May and daughter of General George Barker, an earlier General Officer Commanding British Troops in China, feared for the safety of women arriving in a burgeoning Hong Kong. She campaigned for the establishment of an 'Institute' where women could be safely housed during these times of hectic social and economic change and with the generous help of local businessmen Sir Ellis Kadoorie and Mr Ho Kom Tong, the Club, which took her name, was established in 1916.

The Helena May is an exquisite little Club. It occupies a listed building on Garden Road not far from the entrance to the Peak Tram. This handsome, late Victorian building with its tall ceilings, picture windows, solid parquet floor and hefty wooden architraves has been well maintained and the interior decoration and soft furnishings, as might be expected, have been sympathetically applied. More akin to a London Club in terms of character and facilities, the Helena May has a large, airy dining room, an ante room area with newspapers etc, four private dining rooms and a

Food & Beverages
Main Dining Room
Ante room
4 Private Dining/Function Rooms
Verandah for drinks

Miscellaneous
25,000-book Library
Small WIFI-enabled Computer Room

Accommodation
42 Single and Double Rooms starting at HK$330 per night.

Lounge

Conference room

renowned, 25,000-book library. There is a small, pretty garden with a view of the Peak Tram and a verandah overlooking the garden. It is well supported with over 500 subscribing members and although founded as a club for women, men can, and do join. The Club has 42 accommodation rooms housed in the main building or in the annex which have a 94 per cent occupancy rate with rooms starting at HK$330 per night: long term planning is essential. Access to the Club is easiest by taxi: a five-minute ride from Central, or by Public Light Bus. There are no parking spaces at the Club. The only drawback to the Helena May from the point of view of the visitor is the small reciprocity list. However, being acquainted with a Club member may enable non-reciprocating visitors to gain temporary membership for the small sum of HK$400 per month for a limited period.

To their credit, the 15 female members of the Council ensure that the Club sticks to the founding principles of providing a safe and secure environment for visiting and resident women and of furthering social services, aims to which Lady May devoted so much time and enthusiasm. In so doing, they have created a lovely little Club, welcoming to both sexes, a haven in the middle of Hong Kong and quite the perfect place to escape to and enjoy some peace, some tranquility and an extremely good lunch.

RECIPROCAL CLUBS

UK
City University Club
The University Women's Club

Australia
Lyceum Club (Melbourne)

Library

Hong Kong Football Club

HKFC football field

The Hong Kong Football Club deserves inclusion in this guide because it is so utterly Hong Kong in its sheer enormity and in the lavish, money-(almost)-no-object approach to its 1990's rebuild. Every number is huge from the 700,000 sq ft (yes, that's 700 average Chelsea flats) of useable space to the 240 full-time staff and the club caters to nearly every conceivable legal need. It has to be seen, even if the size of the place is not quite your thing.

The Club began, in a rather more modest way, in 1886. It was founded by James Lockhart, former Registrar General of Hong Kong and Colonial Secretary 'to consist of members proposed

3 Sports Road
Happy Valley
Hong Kong

Tel: +852 2830 9500
Fax: +852 2882 5040

www.hkfc.com.hk
Email: front desk@hkfc.com

Part of the clubhouse in the background

Swimming pool by night

and seconded in the usual way and with a subscription sufficient to cover the cost of balls and tea for the ladies' which rather set the sporting and social tone of the Club for the future.

Lockhart played Association and Rugby Football and the Club fostered both: rugby was played on Saturdays and soccer on Sundays. During WW2, many members were killed in the battle for Hong Kong serving with the Hong Kong Volunteer Defence Corps and there is something rather poignant in the fact that the club now occupies part of the former site of the Corps successor, the Royal Hong Kong Regiment (the Volunteers),

Food & Beverages
The Restaurant
Coffee Shop
Poolside Servery
Sportsman's Bar
Captain's Bar
The Chairman's Bar
The Lounge

Sports facilities
7 Squash Courts
6 Tennis Courts
2 Bowling Greens

Gymnasium
Swimming Pool Complex
Golf Simulators
Snooker Room

Miscellaneous
Beauty and Massage Facilities
Sauna and Steam Rooms
Library
Children's Indoor Play Area

Founder James Haldane Stewart Lockhart (left); one of the stained glass windows in the club (facing page)

itself now disbanded post the 1997 handover to China. After the war, the Club reformed and surviving members returned to find a clubhouse which had been used by the Japanese for stabling mules and a playing area covered in granite chippings from a monument built by the Japanese Army to 'the everlasting glory of the Imperial Japanese Empire'. Fortunately not too everlasting, as it turned out, and play resumed in 1946.

The Club never was the richest. Their main asset was a rather good site in Happy Valley which, very happily for the Club, suddenly found itself in the way of the Royal Hong Kong Jockey Club's expansion plans in the 1990s. The Jockey Club wanted to lengthen their racetrack and the Football Club was in the way. The Jockey Club was awash with cash and the Football Club wasn't. All very fortunate.

The upshot was a spectacular new Clubhouse for the Football Club opened by Governor Chris Patten, complete with every conceivable sports facility save perhaps a ski slope.

The Clubhouse is vast. Think of it more as a Club Village than a Club house. The 2,600 members could comfortably fit, if they so wished, inside the 2,750 capacity stadium which lies inside the racetrack, accessible by tunnel from the main Club. They have 7 exhibition-standard squash courts, 6 tennis courts on the roof, a gymnasium which is eye level with the race track, 4 swimming pools, 2 lawn bowling greens and so on and so on until the mind boggles. It is perfectly possible to become lost.

They take their rugby seriously here and the famous Hong Kong Sevens began at the HKFC in 1976 and they also started the

Rugby 10s. Tragically, the Club lost 11 sporting members in the Bali bombings and there is a touching memorial to these poor souls at the Club.

There are bars everywhere, the most fun being the Sportsman's bar, also inside the race track just yards from the galloping horses and the smartest being the Captain's Bar which looks out over the racetrack. There is a very smart, formal restaurant, a coffee shop serving Asian and Western food and a servery by the pool.

The Club has, luxury of luxuries, boxes at both Happy Valley and Sha Tin race tracks—there is little to beat dinner in one of these with a winning ticket in your pocket. As a reciprocating visitor, it is possible to find space in one of these boxes—ask the Club for help.

The Club has no accommodation but they have a deal with 2 local hotels at discounted rates. Contact the General Manager's office for information which will be provided but they point out, fairly enough, that they will provide the information but not broker a deal for you!

The Club is a 5-minute cab ride from Times Square MTR station or a 15-minute cab ride from Central. There is parking for 170 cars. Somewhere in the vastness, there's probably also a helipad.

RECIPROCAL CLUBS

UK
City University Club
The National Liberal Club
New Club, Cheltenham
Oxford and Cambridge Club
Royal Northern and University Club
The Western Club
Wig & Pen Club

Thailand
The British Club
The Royal Bangkok Sports Club

Malaysia
Penang Club
Penang Sports Club
Penang Swimming Club
Royal Lake Club
Royal Selangor Club

Singapore
The British Club
The Tanglin Club

Australia
Canberra Club
The Naval, Military and Air Force Club
The Royal Automobile Club (Melbourne)
The Royal Automobile Club (Sydney)
The Western Australia Club

New Zealand
The Dunedin Club

Part of another stained glass window

Ladies' Recreation Club

Club entrance

The Ladies' Recreation Club (LRC) is perched, in typical Hong Kong fashion, half way up a seemingly impossibly steep hill on Hong Kong Island. The Club was founded in 1883 when a Mrs Coxon and 18 other ladies petitioned the Governor to grant them some land where they could escape the heat with the children. The (very Victorian) reply from the Governors' office was: 'The ladies should certainly be encouraged in their commendable desire for exercise: I approve'. Presumably taking the ladies at their word, the land granted was several hundred feet above sea level, cooler therefore of course, but accessible only on foot. The Governor's wife, Lady Bowen, formally opened the Club a year later in 1884. From the outset the Club was a success, being

10 Old Peak Road
Hong Kong

Tel: +852 3199 3500
Fax: +852 2840 1478

www.lrc.com.hk
Email: inquiries@lrc.com.hk

One of the tennis courts

View of the tennis courts looking towards the terrace on the right

mentioned favourably in Rudyard Kipling's *From Sea to Sea and Other Sketches* published in 1888. In the early days the Club had a small pavilion and 4 tennis courts on terraces hewn from the side of the hill, with the first Clubhouse being built in 1915. Various improvements took place over the years until the ravages of WW2 and Japanese Occupation during which all of the Club's historical records were destroyed. Members returned in 1945 to 'a car park and a slag heap'.

Under the guidance of an excellent committee of dedicated women however, the Club recovered and has grown over the years into a tremendous family recreation club with over 2,500 members. Whilst there are similar excellent clubs in Hong Kong, the LRC merits inclusion in this guide because it

Food & Beverages
Family Club House
Bistro
Dining Room
Sports Bar
Cocktail Bar

Sports facilities
11 Tennis Courts (when the new block is complete)
2 Squash Courts

2 large Swimming Pools, one indoor and one outdoor
Gymnasium
2 Badminton Courts
A 10-pin Bowling Alley

Miscellaneous
Library
Beauty Salon: the 'Sanctuary'
Pilates/Aerobics Studio
Spa

provides, completely, every sporting or culinary diversion which an overheated or fractious visiting family could possibly need at a site just minutes from the main residential and hotel areas behind Central. It would be an easy thing to spend the entire day at the LRC, either as a couple or as a family and not want for something to do and without being under each other's feet the whole time.

At the time of writing, the Club has just finished undergoing a radical rebuild which will see a new block built on the footprint of just one tennis court (so Hong Kong!). This will still leave nine tennis courts along with the squash courts, gymnasium, badminton courts, pilates and aerobics studios and indoor and outdoor swimming pools. And as if that were not enough, the new building will house a ten-pin bowling alley, an expanded library and, being the second reason for the LRCs inclusion, a new Spa, the consultants for which also advised the Mandarin and Four Seasons Hotels Spas. Prices will be sub-market and demand will be strong.

There is a smart dining room, a family clubhouse which is ideal with the brood in tow, a sports bar and a cocktail bar. The nicest spot to have lunch is the Verandah, which looks down over the tennis courts towards the harbour.

The Club is a sanctuary for visitors to Hong Kong and for residents alike and if visiting Hong Kong with children, it is ideal. As with so many Hong Kong Clubs there is no accommodation but the General Managers office will advise where good reciprocal deals might be had. The Club lies at the end of an interestingly steep 5-minute cab ride from Admiralty and Central MTR stations.

RECIPROCAL CLUBS

Canada
Vancouver Lawn Tennis
& Badminton Club

UK
The Hurlingham Club
Oxford and Cambridge Club

Thailand
The British Club

Malaysia
Penang Swimming Club

Singapore
The British Club
The Tanglin Club

Australia
City Tattersalls Club
The Royal Automobile Club
Royal South Yarra Lawn Tennis Club

Royal Hong Kong Yacht Club

An aerial view of Kellett Island

The earliest recorded competitive water sports in Hong Kong/ China took place on the Pearl River in the 1830s when members of the Canton Rowing Club rowed the 93 miles to Hong Kong, bravely running the gauntlet of the feared and rather too active, Pearl River pirates. They competed with the Hong Kong Boat Club based at North Point on the Island and many interport races took place over the next several decades. Organised sailing however, appears not to have begun formally until 1890, when the Hong Kong Corinthian Sailing Club was founded, the aim of which was to 'better manage the racing of Mersey Canoes'. In 1894, the Lords of the Admiralty approved the change of name to the Royal Hong Kong Yacht Club and the Club, as it is constituted now, came into

Kellett Island
Causeway Bay
Hong Kong

Tel: +852 2832 2817
Fax: +852 2572 5399
www.rhkyc.org.hk
Email: info@rhkyc.org.hk

Shelter Cove bar

Pool with view towards Central

being. The RHKYC moved to its present site on Kellett Island in 1938, the Clubhouse being built on the foundations of the old Naval gunpowder magazine. The Club was used, and sadly abused, by the occupying Japanese during the War but was then reopened to as much fanfare as could be mustered by surviving members and by Officers and ratings from HMS Vengeance in September 1945 (the Club proudly displays in its wonderful bar, the original Vengeance Ships plaque, donated by the Captain and crew).

Do not, by the way, look for an island: Kellett Island itself is no longer an actual island, a causeway having been built to it from Hong Kong Island back in 1951. Indeed as the years have passed and the harbour has shrunk due to reclamation, Kellett Island has

Food & Beverages
Compass Room: fine dining

Kellett Island
Bistro: family restaurant
Main Bar
Bar

Middle Island
Indoor and Outdoor Restaurants
Barbecue Area
Shelter Cove
Casual Dining Room
Bar

Sports facilities
Sailing at all three sites; gymnasium; 2 Squash Courts

Kellett Island
25-yard Swimming Pool; Bowling Alley

Accommodation
The Club does not have its own accommodation but it has corporate deals with both the Excelsior and Park Lane Hotels, each being a three-minute taxi ride from Kellett Island. Speak to the Club Office for details.

Middle Island clubhouse

very firmly become part of Hong Kong side but it still somehow manages to retain its very separate feel.

And what a tremendous feel that is: the RHKYC is a superb club. With 3,850 Hong Kong members and 9,000 absent members it is well supported and very well funded. This large Club (3 sites) is efficiently managed and has the confident, casual air of a club very comfortable in its own skin. The main Clubhouse at Kellett Island has stunning views out over Victoria Harbour towards Kowloon and beyond towards Tai Mo Shan, the Territory's tallest mountain. It is a classic 1930s building with lovely wide verandahs, a fantastically convivial bar, first-rate dining facilities and tons of room to breathe. There is ample space in the grounds in which to enjoy both the (somewhat illusory) solitude and the 180-degree views of the harbour. For smart dining, go to the Compass Room on the first floor. With a family in tow, try the Bistro on the ground floor with its terraces overlooking the harbour. For a drink, either the wonderful bar or its adjacent verandahs overlooking the harbour. There is a reading room, the Chart Room, where all the local newspapers are provided. Sports facilities include 2 squash courts, a swimming pool and a gymnasium. Kellett Island is a marvellous place to spend a day and is perfect for dinner: no hotel on Hong Kong Island can compete for location. The Club is a five-minute taxi ride from Causeway Bay MTR or, for the romantic, a three-minute sampan ride over the water from Gloucester Road.

A twenty-minute taxi ride away on the south side of Hong Kong Island and a few hundred yards off the headland between Deepwater Bay and Repulse Bay, lies the Middle Island Clubhouse. Access is via a sampan (hail them from the beach). The Clubhouse and facilities were renovated in 2003 and are in great condition. There is another excellent bar, indoor and outdoor restaurants, a private beach and yet again, views, views, views. This is where much of the serious dinghy sailing takes place with Lasers, Wanderers and Optimists being the most popular classes. Middle

Island is 'Swallows and Amazons' country: beautiful, secluded, a lovely spot and the perfect place to spend a day away from the noise of Central.

The Club's rural offshoot is Shelter Cove located just off Hirams Highway on the way to Sai Kung. Shelter Cove is primarily a base for cruising boats but is also a lovely escape for day visitors coming out of the city to the magnificent Sai Kung Country Park with its bays, inlets and jungle-clad hills. It is a 15-minute walk from the nearest bus stop and the bus ride from Kowloon will take a little over half an hour. Both green (New Territories) and red (Island) taxis will take you there in about 30 minutes from Kowloon or 45 minutes from Hong Kong Island. There is a bar with a terrace, a casual dining room and a barbecue area.

All three locations are children-friendly and all lie within secure, safe grounds. This highly prestigious, smoothly run Club offers the reciprocating visitor practically everything he could ask for, save accommodation, but the Club has deals with two good, nearby hotels which are detailed on page 41.

RECIPROCAL CLUBS
Unsurprisingly, for a Club of this quality, numerous. Practically every sailing club of note in the UK, Asia and Australia have reciprocal arrangements with the RHKYC. Here are a few:

Canada
Royal Canadian Yacht Club
Royal Nova Scotia Yacht Squadron
Royal Vancouver Yacht Club
Royal Victoria Yacht Club

UK
Leander Club
The Naval Club
Royal Air Force Yacht Club
Royal Corinthian Yacht Club
Royal Cornwall Yacht Club
Royal Thames Yacht Club

South Africa
Gordon's Bay Yacht Club
Royal Cape Yacht Club

Thailand
Royal Varuna Yacht Club

Singapore
Changi Sailing Club

Australia
The Naval & Military Club Melbourne
Royal Brighton Yacht Club
Royal Geelong Yacht Club
Royal Melbourne Yacht Squadron
Royal Perth Yacht Club

New Zealand
Royal New Zealand Yacht Club
Royal Port Nicholson Yacht Club

Kellett Island clubhouse main entrance

United Services Recreation Club

Club entrance

The former British Garrison's families Club, the United Services Recreation Club (USRC), lies on nearly five acres of prime land opposite Kings Park at the junction of Jordan and Gascoigne Roads in the Jordan District of Kowloon. Founded in 1911 to provide sports and social facilities for the Royal Artillery stationed in nearby Gun Club Hill Barracks, the Club has played host down the years to generations of British Servicemen, their wives and children and was for those in quarters nearby, an integral part of family life. The USRC had always been something of a lifeline for those living in downtown Kowloon, serving in either Osborne or Gun Club Barracks or at the Queen Elizabeth Military Hospital. For them, living miles from the rural quiet of the New Territories

1 Gascoigne Road
Kings Park
Kowloon
Hong Kong

Tel: +852 2367 0672
Fax: +852 2724 0949
www.usrc.org.hk
Email: info@usrc.org.hk

Staircase to the upper floor

Main clubhouse and pool

where much of the British Army was stationed, the USRC was a green lung and refuge from the cheek-by-jowl proximity of teeming humanity and impossible traffic in one of the most densely populated cities in the world. It was also where many, having 'marched out' of quarters at the end of their two-year tour, spent their last, wistful evening in the tropics, before the next day's rather more prosaic experience of jumping into a Gurkha Transport Regiment minibus, bound for Kai Tak Airport and the flight back to England.

As late as 1995, still over 60 per cent of the members were Servicemen, including by then, Gurkhas who had moved into Gun Club from Sek Kong Village up in the New Territories near

Food & Beverages
Venetian Café: family coffee shop with Asian and Western food
Poolside Café
Grill Room: delightful; overlooks the pool
Oceania Lounge: 'rattan infused' as the Club themselves describe it
Gunner's Bar: mahogany; space to move and umpteen plaques from Regiments which have belonged over the years

Sports facilities
Driving Range; Putting Green; Gymnasium; 3 Swimming Pools; 4 Tennis Courts (floodlit); Squash Courts (with aircon); Lawn Bowls

Accommodation
The Club has 6 no smoking, double or family rooms, each with aircon, TV, VCD, en suite shower and loo, fridge and safe box. Rates vary from HK$480 to HK$550 per night with discounts for stays in excess of 7 nights.

Regimental plaque

the border with China. Despite an earlier civilian recruitment drive in anticipation of the handover of Hong Kong back to the Chinese Government, the consequent withdrawal of British forces came as a membership blow to the Club, and numbers have only just crept back over 700. The Club is now firmly back on its feet again however, numbers are increasing and once more it 'feels' right. The location is excellent, situated as the Club is on the north east corner of the shopping mecca of Tsim Tsha Shui in the middle of Kowloon, whilst at the same time protected from the hustle and bustle within its own green cordon sanitaire. There is room enough to breathe here and space enough to find a little solitude and after a day shopping on Nathan Road, it feels like a sanctuary.

In the centre of the grounds, away from the busy roads is the solid, unfussy main building. Do not look for grand colonial architecture here: this is good old practical Public Works Department (PWD) stuff—if you grew up in any of Britain's former colonies you will recognise it straightaway—and of course, it works. The Clubhouse has high ceilings, hardwood floors and picture windows which look out over the swimming pool and the grounds. It is well maintained, bright and cheerful. On the first floor is the Oceania Lounge, a bar where you can choose from a very good menu before dining in the adjacent Grill Room which is small and intimate, and where the food is excellent. You need remind yourself that you are indeed in Hong Kong, when you see at the far end of the Grill Room an open fire, installed by the ever thoughtful PWD, for those two or three evenings per year when the temperature drops to what would be considered a heat wave in Hampshire. The Venetian Café on the ground floor has a varied, simple menu, is more casual and is ideal with small children in tow. The recently renovated Gunner's Bar contains some fascinating old Regimental plaques and photographs and is generally full. The sports facilities,

Gunner's Bar

though not Olympic standard, are fine, with well-maintained tennis courts, squash courts, gymnasium, swimming pool and children's paddling pools. The Club has six accommodation rooms in a separate, bunker-like building, on the northern, Jordan Road side of the Club, which are clean, comfortable and perfectly adequate but not plush: this is reflected in the price. The website contains a link to the club's *In Bloom* Magazine and hyperlinks to most of the 84 reciprocating clubs. The USRC is an uncomplicated, comfortable, family-friendly little club with a nostalgic whiff of the British Army about it and is an entire world away from nearby, new Kowloon hotels. Access is easy either by red (Kowloon) or green (New territories) taxi or by MTR to the nearby Jordan Station which is a five-minute walk. There is free parking for 70 cars.

RECIPROCAL CLUBS

Canada
The Union Club of British Columbia

UK
The Army and Navy Club
Bath and Country Club
The Carlton Club
The Commonwealth Club
The Lansdowne Club
The Naval and Military Club
The New Cavendish Club
The New Club
St. James's Club
Royal Scots Club
Wig and Pen Club

Zimbabwe
Harare Club

Kenya
The Mombasa Club

South Africa
Cape Town Club
Durban Club

Thailand
The British Club

Malaysia
Penang Club
The Royal Commonwealth Society
Royal Ipoh Club
Royal Port Dickson Yacht Club

Singapore
Hollandse Club

Australia
The Canberra Club
The Naval and Military Club
The Naval, Military and Air Force Club
The Royal Automobile Club
Royal Exchange
United Service Club
The Western Australian Club

New Zealand
The Dunedin Club
The Wellington Club

THAILAND

The British Club
The Royal Bangkok Sports Club
Royal Varuna Yacht Club

A 20th-century impression of Royal Bangkok Sports Club (above);
View down the fairway at The Royal Bangkok Sports Club
(previous pages)

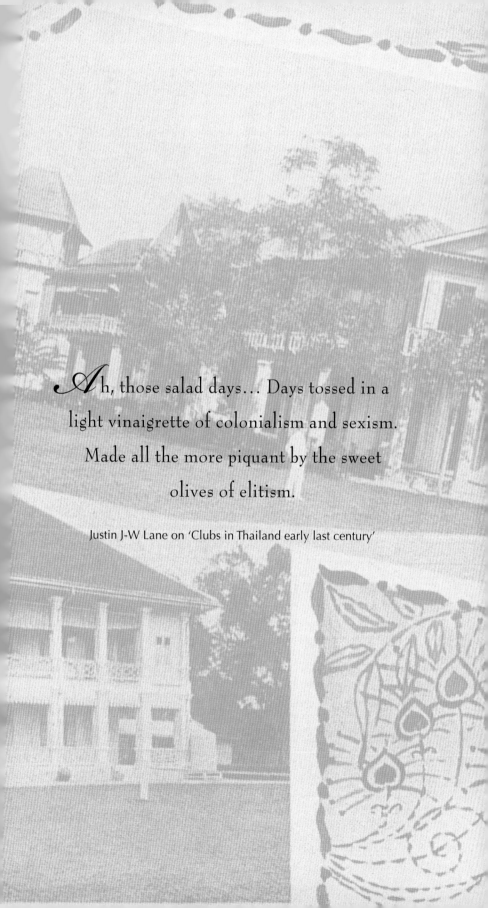

Ah, those salad days… Days tossed in a
light vinaigrette of colonialism and sexism.
Made all the more piquant by the sweet
olives of elitism.

Justin J-W Lane on 'Clubs in Thailand early last century'

The British Club

Main clubhouse

As a general rule it was trade, followed by formal colonisation, which brought large numbers of Europeans to Asia. Thailand was different. At the turn of the last century Bangkok was already a major port, described in WA Graham's *Siam*, published in 1912, as being 'the largest city in all Further India having a population of over 350,000'. Teak from the northern forests and from the borders with Burma attracted the traders but dextrous diplomacy by King Rama V prevented colonisation. Despite there being no colonial power, there were, by 1912, over 1,000 Europeans living in the capital, most of whom were British and nearly all of whom were involved, in one way or another, with teak. The British Club was founded in 1903 by the earlier arrivals

189 Surawong Road
Silom
Bangkok 10500
Thailand

Tel: +662 234 0247
Fax: +662 236 1560

www.britishclubbangkok.org
Email: britclub@loxinfo.co.th

One of the tennis courts

Swimming pool with clubhouse in the background

of this British contingent, most of whom were businessmen working for one of the great banking or teak trading houses such as The Hong Kong and Shanghai Banking Corporation, which opened for business in Bangkok in 1888, Anglo-Thai, The Borneo Company or the Bombay Trading Company. Louis T Leonowens, the son of Anna of *The King and I* fame was one of those founders (and a rather busy one: he was also the owner of the Oriental Hotel, now considered by many travel writers to be the best hotel in the world). As the British Club was largely a business club, sportsmen tended to join The Royal Bangkok Sports Club and it was not until 1919 that the Club bought two tennis courts from the Siam Electricity Company which lay on adjacent land. Thereafter, the nature of the Club began to change as younger men joined and formed sports teams, travelling to places such as Chiang Mai in the north to compete with teams from the Gymkhana Club. The Club prospered and grew and by the 1930's was considered to be one of the cornerstones

Food & Beverages
Verandah Bar: Thai and Western food; children-friendly
Churchill Bar: casual
The Sala: Thai and Western food

Sports facilities
4 Tennis Courts
3 Squash Courts
Gymnasium
30-yard Swimming Pool
Children's Pool
Billiards Room

Miscellaneous
Thai Massage
Reading Room

Accommodation
The Club can arrange discounted accommodation for visitors at the Narai Hotel beginning at Bt2,200 per night or at the 222 Hotel, one of the smart new micro hotels which have opened in Bangkok beginning at Bt2,900 per night. Both are good hotels and are within 2 minutes' walk from the Club.

Aerial view of the clubhouse (above)

of British expatriate life along with The English Church, the Bangkok Nursing Home, the Neilson Hays Library and the bar at the Oriental Hotel on the River Menam (Chao Praya).

Whilst for decades a purely British Club, in post war years, membership, whether voting or non voting, has gradually opened to all races, as had been the case at the Royal Bangkok Sports Club from inception.

The British Club now typifies the transition which many clubs have successfully made from being purely gentlemen's clubs to family recreation clubs. Membership stands at 1,100, approximately half of whom are British but with 39 other nationalities being represented in the membership, it is a truly multinational club.

The Club lies on a quiet, green, 3-acre plot, in the middle of what has become the busy shopping and nightlife area of Silom. It is happily cocooned however, from the sometimes extreme hustle and bustle by its boundaries which give the Club something of the feel of an oasis in what is a fairly frenzied, urban environment. Access is easy either by taxi or by the elevated train system to the nearby Chong Nonsi Station. Parking is ample. The Clubhouse is a beautiful, late Edwardian building surrounded by grass, palm trees and rain trees. Maintenance standards of this old building are high and the recently renovated façade is impressive. The management undertakes continuous renovation projects around both the club and the grounds, generally ensuring a high standard of service and facilities.

The Club is well managed, the food, particularly Thai, is good and the sports facilities are more than ample with four hard tennis courts, three squash courts, a gymnasium and a lovely pool. Accommodation is not available, but the Club has

an excellent arrangement with two local hotels to provide rooms at discounted rates. Both are within very easy walking distance. Next door to the club, almost as an annex, is the Neilson Hayes Library, one of the few listed buildings in Bangkok. The library owns a huge, varied and valuable collection of travel and historical books on Asia which can be read in the library for a token sum: ideal for the visitor transiting through Bangkok to other parts of the East. The British Club is an ideal place at which to base yourself prior to shopping and sightseeing forays or simply to spend the day by the pool. It is a safe, children-friendly club, easy to find and inexpensive and with a larger than average long term membership, most of whom are happy to share their accrued local knowledge with visitors.

RECIPROCAL CLUBS

CANADA
Edmonton Petroleum Club
Hollyburn Country Club
Montefiore Club (Montreal)
The Mount Royal Club (Montreal)
National Club (Ontario)
Ontario Club
Rideau Tennis Club (Ontario)
St. James's Club (Montreal)

UK
Caledonian Club
City University Club
The Lansdowne Club
National Liberal Club
The Naval and Military Club
The Naval Club
The Nottingham & Nottinghamshire
United Service Club
Royal Air Force Club
The Royal Automobile Club
Royal Northern and University Club
Royal Scots Club
St. James's Club (Manchester)
St. James's Club (London)
United Oxford & Cambridge
University Club
Wig and Pen Club

HONG KONG
Hong Kong Cricket Club
Hong Kong Football Club
The Kowloon Cricket Club
Ladies' Recreation Club
United Services Recreation Club

MALAYSIA
Penang Club
Penang Sports Club
Penang Swimming Club
Royal Commonwealth Society
Royal Ipoh Club
Royal Lake Club

SINGAPORE
The British Club
Singapore Cricket Club
The Tanglin Club

AUSTRALIA
Athenaeum Club
The Canberra Club
Melbourne Savage Club
The Naval and Military Club
The Naval, Military and Air Force Club
North Queensland Club
The Royal Automobile Club
United Service Club

NEW ZEALAND
The Christchurch Club
The Dunedin Club
The Hamilton Club
The Northern Club

Surawong Road entrance

The Royal Bangkok Sports Club

New clubhouse

Take the Skytrain north from Saladaeng Station in the Silom area of Bangkok, and as the train begins to run up Ratchadamri Road towards Siam Square, look to your left out over the huge expanse of green, which comes into view as the train begins to gather speed. These are the magnificent grounds of The Royal Bangkok Sports Club and the green which you see is an 18-hole golf course, contained within a horse-racing track, all lying within just a few minutes' walk from the centre of town. The Royal Bangkok Sports Club (RBSC) is indeed one of the richest, most politically well-connected, most lavishly equipped Clubs in Asia. That it occupies such a huge piece of land, smack in the middle of Bangkok's central business district and so close to most of the major hotels, gives an indication of both its standing and of its wealth. Thai society aspires to belong to the RBSC and

1 Henri Dunant Street
Pathumwan
Bangkok 10330
Thailand

Tel: +662 652 5000
Fax: +662 255 4158

www.rbsc.org
Email: sportsclub@rbsc.org

The old clubhouse

Tennis courts with olympic-sized pool beyond

works extremely hard to get there and the exclusivity enjoyed by the 9,600 members is actively and jealously guarded by both the members themselves and by the management. A day at the RBSC is without doubt, an experience.

The RBSC has quite a history. It began life as a racing club at the end of the 19th century when Franklin Hurst, an Englishman, wrote to the Minister for Foreign Affairs asking permission to set up a sports field and race track in Bangkok. The King promptly agreed, granting a lease at the present site in Sri Pathumwan. Hurst soon dropped out of the picture however, going off to run the Oriental Hotel with Louis Leonowens (son of Anna from *Anna and the King*), but the nascent committee had the bit between its teeth: a list of members was drawn up and racing began almost immediately, and from 1901, golf.

Food & Beverages
Air Bar
Main Dining Room
Fast Food Terrace
Snack Bar
Swimming Pool Bar
Verandah Terrace
Winning Post Restaurant

Sports facilities
5 Badminton Courts
1 Basketball Court
18-Hole Golf Course
Horse-Racing Track

2 Running Tracks
Lawn Bowls
Gymnasium
4 Squash Courts
6 Tennis Courts
3 Swimming Pools

Miscellaneous
Barber Shop
Beauty Salon
Reading Room
Sauna
Spa

Walkway towards the old clubhouse

Bangkok was still a small city in those days and the Club lay well away from the then centre of town (New Road), on the edge of what was still lush countryside, complete with wildlife. In his memoirs, S Conyer-Keyes, an Englishman, then resident in Bangkok, describes how 'they shot snipe on the golf course on Saturday evenings, one drawback being that almost all of the shot landed on the first green... and the cascades of falling shot added an unusual feature to the niceties of the putt'. There were lots of 'firsts' here. In 1911, the first aircraft seen in Thailand landed in the middle of the racetrack, piloted by French flyer Charles van den Born who flew for the wonderfully named Societe d'Aviation d'Extreme Oriental. So impressed was the King with this feat that three potential pilots were promptly sent to France, returning two years later, fully trained and complete with aircraft. Thus the Royal Thai Airforce was born, although the Club members probably did not envisage it headquartering itself in the middle of the racetrack for the next six months.

After the bleak years of the 1930s and 1940s, with Thailand's painful transition from a system of absolute to constitutional monarchy and the ravages of WW2, came a gradually increasing post war prosperity. Club membership quadrupled, partly as a result of an increasing American presence in Bangkok. Two of

The swimming pool (above); a panaromic view of the club grounds (below)

these new members were ex-OSS men, Jim Thompson, who went on to found the world renowned Thai silk business bearing his name and Alexander MacDonald, who went on to found the Bangkok Post. MacDonald's sympathetic and evocative description of a changing Thailand during this period will ring true for many who have lived in the Far East: 'Bangkok was an intriguing clutter of old and new, east and west. As a community, it tried on the things of modern civilisation—electric power, fast autos, telephones and public health campaigns—like a women trying on hats, oftentimes giggled at their absurdity and discarded them, relaxing to more informal ways of life'.

By the 1970s, Bangkok had become a large, cosmopolitan as well as fun-loving city. Thailand's economy was growing, the expatriate population was on the increase and the RBSC had become a core component of a busy and highly social way of life. It is a great Club. There is little, in fact, that the RBSC does not offer. Every conceivable sport, dish or drink is available somewhere at the RBSC or in its 'annex', the sister Royal Bangkok Polo Club, located two miles' distant near Lumpini Park. Where else in the world can you play 18 holes of golf in the morning, cool off in an Olympic-size swimming pool before lunch, then watch an afternoon's horse racing, all in the middle

Garden with fountain

of a city? And should the Club, as you sit there in the Winning Post Dining Room surrounded by the great and the good of Thailand, strike you as just a tad formal, just remember that the nude sunbathing and rather racy squash court and top diving-board lovemaking scenes in the book *Emmanuelle* actually took place at the RBSC, although the author, a Frenchman working for the United Nations, adequately disguises this fact in the text! There, the Club has the lot.

The Club is a two-minute taxi ride from Siam Square Skytrain station and a 10-minute ride from Silom and Sathorn Roads. There is parking for 725 cars. There is no accommodation and sadly no corporate deals with local hotels. It is probably assumed that you possess your own penthouse. That minor hiccup apart, definitely a must-visit if you are in Bangkok.

RECIPROCAL CLUBS

UK
The Royal Automobile Club

Hong Kong
Hong Kong Cricket Club
Hong Kong Football Club
Hong Kong Golf Club
The Kowloon Cricket Club

Malaysia
Penang Sports Club
Royal Lake Club
Royal Selangor Club

Singapore
Singapore Cricket Club
The Tanglin Club

Australia
City Tattersalls Club
Royal Perth Golf Club
Tattersall's Club

The RBSC club crest

CLUB CLASS
IN
ASIA PACIFIC

The Insiders' Guide to Private Members' Clubs

An insiders' guide to an elite selection of private members' clubs linked by history and character.

Written on the basis of personal experience and observation, this informative guide provides detailed descriptions, listings of facilities as well as contact details for clubs ranging from the Foreign Correspondents Club in Hong Kong to The Penang Club in Malaysia, The United Service Club in Brisbane to the Tanglin Club in Singapore.

" Club Class in Asia Pacific offers club members practical, unique and fascinating alternatives to the ubiquitous chains. "

www.clubclassguides.com

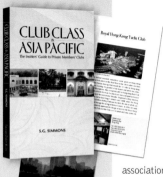

If you are looking at taking a trip to Asia Pacific this wonderful guide is the ideal travelling companion those wishing to find a character alternative to the endless chains.

Throughout the world there is a unique network of private members clubs each with their own special appeal, partly for their elegance and personal service at reasonable price and partly for their historical associations. These clubs provided social cohes to expatriate European communities during the colonial era, and are looked back on with huge affection and nostalgia. Today, modernised and updated, they continue to thrive.

Club Class in Asia Pacific presents you with detailed, fascinating and informative guide into a chosen few of these clubs.

The book includes detailed profiles describing the premises, features of architectural interes history of the club and its membership, plus current facilities and character. Each entry also has beautiful colour photographs as well as full contact details.

In addition, there is an invaluable list of clubs worldwide with reciprocal arrangements.

Even if you don't have immediate plans to travel to Asia Pacific this guide still provides a fascinating and entertaining insight into the history and tradition of the private members' club

Contents includes:

Introduction

Clubs in...

- Hong Kong
- Singapore
- Thailand
- Malaysia
- Australia
- New Zealand

Plus Worldwide
Reciprocal Club Listings

Royal Varuna Yacht Club

The clubhouse

The setting of The Royal Varuna Yacht Club is quite simply, stunning. It lies on the point between Pattaya and Jomtien beaches, 85 miles southeast of Bangkok and 1¼ hours from the new Suvarnaphumi Airport, in its own 6 acres of land complete with private beach and uninterrupted views out over deep blue sea, towards the island of Koh Larn in the Gulf of Siam. Given population growth and the explosion in beachside land prices, it is unlikely that all but the richest could afford to purchase the Varuna's site now. Happily, the club was founded nearly 50 years ago in a different financial age and today's members, and visitors, benefit enormously.

The Club was founded in 1957 after an advertisement appeared in the Bangkok Post in April of that year seeking 'like-minded

286 Pratamnak Road
Pattaya
Chonburi 20150
Thailand

Tel: +663 830 6290
Fax: +663 825 0115

www.royal-varuna-yacht-club.com
Email: office@royal-varuna-yacht-club.com

Swimming pool with Koh Larn Island in the distance

The private beach

friends to form a boating club'. One of this group of friends was Prince Bhisadij Rajani, an advisor to King Bhumibol, who himself began to sail at the Club in 1960 and whose patronage certainly helped in the early days. At first, the members sailed in a motley collection of Enterprises, Ospreys, a folkboat and a sailing canoe. Membership grew as Bangkokians, escaping from the heat of the city each weekend, headed southeast over the Bang Pa Kong River and the Club prospered. The 1960s were great years for the Varuna. The King often sailed in his own Enterprise 'Rajpatan' (Royal Pattern), which he built largely himself, on one occasion sailing against, amongst others, Prince Phillip who was visiting Thailand, in a race from Varuna to Koh Larn. The King won and Prince Phillip, notwithstanding a distinguished Royal Navy past, came 21st out of-well-21! Back at the clubhouse the King would often form part of an impromptu quartet in which he played the saxophone accompanied by Maurice Rocco from the Oriental Hotel and such others who were musical and perhaps unafraid of getting their notes wrong. The Club continued to grow and prosper, hosting the sailing competition of the 1967 South East Asia Peninsula Games, when the King took a joint Gold Medal with his daughter, 16-year-old Princess Ubolratana. In the last

Food & Beverages
Lower Deck: restaurant and bar
with Asian and Western food
Beach Bar: weekends only
Members' Lounge: snacks, TV etc

Sports facilities
Excellent Sailing Facilities
Boat Hire
Sailing Tuition
A 25-yard Swimming Pool
Children's Pool

Accommodation
19 rooms, the most expensive being
Bt560 per night. Not in the least
ritzy but clean and comfortable.
Book early for weekends. Not all air-
conditioned but all have fans (and a
sea breeze!).

Single and family accommodation rooms (above); dining area (right)

20 years, four World Championships have been held at the club, testament to its facilities and to the quality of the sailing in the waters of the Gulf of Siam. Members now sail Hobie Cats, Lasers, Enterprises and Optimists and of the 450 members, over 100 are enthusiastic sailors. Members and visitors can hire boats and sailing instruction is available at very affordable rates. The Varuna is a gem and several expatriates have moved to Pattaya for no other reason than they wished to be near the centre of their sporting and social lives.

You need visit only once to understand why. The new clubhouse, opened in January 2005 by the Crown Prince, is immaculate. Cool breezes blow through the open lower deck of the building providing relief from the often recorded 95°F. Food, both western and Thai, is simple, wholesome and inexpensive. Accommodation is clean and comfortable, if spartan, yet this is a small price to pay for the privilege of enjoying the use of such a beautifully positioned club. A couple of days at the Varuna constitutes a first rate, relaxing holiday in itself but it is also an ideal base from which to explore the Province of Rayong with its beautiful beaches and also further east, towards Cambodia.

RECIPROCAL CLUBS

Canada
Royal Vancouver Yacht Club

UK
Ballyholme Yacht Club
Royal Channel Islands Yacht Club
Royal Dart Yacht Club
Royal Southern Yacht Club

The Netherlands
Royal Netherlands Yacht Club

Seychelles
Seychelles Yacht Club

South Africa
Royal Cape Yacht Club

Hong Kong
Aberdeen Boat Club
Royal Hong Kong Yacht Club

Australia
Middle Harbour Yacht Club
Southport Yacht Club

New Zealand
Bucklands Beach Yacht Club

MALAYSIA

Penang Swimming Club (above); Taiping Club (right) and Penang Sports Club (previous pages)

From a Malayan Verandah

12 O'Clock and 7 hours ahead of English time! The Savoy, the Ritz, the Criterion, Claridges— all the big hotels in London anticipating a joyous crowd to see the old year out and the new year in. And here in the tropics it is 12 O'Clock and a hard, white moon shines brilliantly across quiet green compounds illuminating the bright red polish of the ceiling wax palm, shining through feathery casuarinas, gilding the gleaming tops of coconut palms, outlining the creeping body of a jungle cat as it crawls stealthily along by a hedge of bamboos. 12 O'Clock on a new year's night in the tropics—the light from the English Club can be seen and figures whisking madly to the strains of *Auld Lang Syne*, the women— the majority of them—with thoughts fixed on the little ones at Home, and, because of that, clasping hands the more tightly and whisking more madly, to stifle the pain of separation.

F.M., *Times of Malaya*, Thursday 7th January 1926

Penang Club

Pool with view south and the Pergola restaurant (above); the old Penang Club (facing page)

The lovely island of Penang, or Prince of Wales Island as it was first known, was one of the earliest British settlements in the Far East being founded in 1786 by Captain Francis Light of the Honourable East India Company. The Sultan of Kedah had ceded the island to Light in exchange for 'John Company's' protection from Siamese and Burmese aggression and Province Wellesley, a long strip of coast on the Sultanate of Kedah, was added in 1791. The island's prosperity was based upon the East India Company's need for a naval base in the area to counter growing French ambition and upon the cultivation of coffee and spices, mainly nutmeg and mace. The capital of Penang

42B Jalan Sultan Ahmed Shah
10050 Penang
Malaysia

Tel: +604 227 7366
Fax: +604 227 6804

www.penangclub.org
Email: pgclub@po.jaring.my

The Penang Club crest

The Verandah with dining room above

is George Town, a beautiful, historic town with a tremendous architectural heritage of late Georgian, Victorian and Art Deco buildings. Behind the town lies Penang Hill, accessed by the funicular railway completed in 1923, from where there are stunning views out over the Straits of Malacca towards Province Wellesley. The beaches of Batu Feringhi in the north of the island are lovely, if crowded, but it is George Town which is the pull and in good part the reason for the inclusion of the three Penang Clubs in this book.

The Penang Club was founded in 1868, but its probable forerunner was the Prince of Wales Island Club amongst whose

Food & Beverages
Main Dining Room
Family Dining Room
Dolphin Bar
Men's Bar
Verandah
Pergola Bistro

Sports facilities
2 Squash Courts
Swimming Pool

Miscellaneous
Library
Billiards Room
WIFI facilities

Accommodation
The Club has 6 double rooms and 1 suite, all en suite, each with aircon, TV, mini-bar and safe. Rates for the doubles are RM100 per room.

Pool with view north and the Verandah

original members was Stamford Raffles. Raffles subsequently went on to establish the settlement of Singapore which together with Malacca and Penang, was grouped into the colony of the Straits Settlements in 1826. Penang was occupied by the Japanese in WW2 and the Club was ransacked. All the historical records were lost and the Club and grounds were left in ruins for which the Club was paid the princely sum of 350 Straits Dollars in compensation in 1950!

Originally founded as a gentlemen's club, the Penang Club has tried, with considerable success, to adapt and become a more family-friendly Club over the years although its limited real estate has made this a difficult task in terms of facilities. Also, the Clubhouse is a 1960s rebuild with all the consequent architectural challenges associated with that period but it is well maintained, clean and serviceable. Nevertheless, there is something about the Penang Club which is very attractive. Perhaps it is its history as one of the social centres of this pretty little town or perhaps it is its position on Jalan Sultan Ahmed Shah in a prime spot by the sea where a drink by the water's edge on a warm evening, with the attendant views out over the Straits of Malacca, is a joy. Whatever the reason there is a warm, comfortable feel about the Club, the staff are welcoming

and friendly and it is a tremendous place to base yourself for a week's exploration of George Town.

Unusually for these times, the Club retains a Men's Bar, which is on the ground floor of the building tucked away behind the reception. The mixed bar, the Dolphin Bar, is on the first floor next to which is the main dining room. This has lovely views over the sea. Perhaps the best spot for lunch is the open verandah next to the pool and if you have children in tow, this is where you will be. The Asian food is first rate, particularly the Penang curries. The Pergola Bistro lies at the far end of the pool and serves, primarily, Italian food.

Sports facilities are limited to 2 squash courts and to the swimming pool due to the lack of space. Both are well maintained and serviceable. There is an excellent, 11,000-book library and the Club has installed WIFI internet throughout.

The Club has seven, very good-value accommodation rooms which are clean and comfortable, and which have views out to sea. The Club is a twenty-five minute drive from Penang Airport, a five-minute walk from the E&O Hotel (both Somerset Maugham and Rudyard Kipling stayed there) and a couple of minutes by cab from the centre of town. There is ample parking.

RECIPROCAL CLUBS

Canada
The Union Club of British Columbia

UK
The Army and Navy Club
The Lansdowne Club
The Naval and Military Club
Oriental Club
Oxford and Cambridge Club
Royal Scots Club
The Travellers Club
The Western Club

Zimbabwe
Harare Club

Hong Kong
Hong Kong Cricket Club
Hong Kong Football Club
The Kowloon Cricket Club
United Services Recreation Club

Thailand
The British Club
The Royal Bangkok Sports Club

Malaysia
Royal Selangor Club
Royal Ipoh Club
Royal Lake Club
Royal Port Dickson Yacht Club
Taiping New Club

Singapore
The British Club
Singapore Cricket Club
The Tanglin Club

Australia
The Brisbane Club
The Naval and Military Club
The Royal Automobile Club
Union, University and Schools' Club of Sydney
United Service Club
Tattersall's Club
The Western Australian Club

Penang Sports Club

Clubhouse with Penang Hill in the background

The Penang Sports Club lies on a beautiful, green, 18-acre site in a prime and valuable position in the middle of lovely old Georgetown. It has 3,700 enthusiastic members and is consequently well funded, which fact becomes immediately evident upon visiting. The Club and the grounds are well maintained and there is a pleasing feel of pro-activity about the place with the busy staff engaged in any number of new projects around the Club, the most recent being the installation of a brand new gymnasium. There is a happy, friendly atmosphere here and they make visitors welcome.

Jalan Utama
Penang 10450
Malaysia

Tel: +604 229 4541
Fax: +604 229 2391

www.pgsportsclub.com.my
Email: info@pgsportsclub.com

The Penang Sports Club crest

The pool

Few historical records of the Sports Club remain, most having been lost during the Japanese occupation of WW2, but it is known that it began life in 1900 as the Penang Cricket Club, located on the Esplanade, not far from Fort Cornwallis. It moved to its present site in 1939 to a beautiful building which was originally a Military Hospital treating Indian Army Sepoys wounded in WW1. Once the new General Hospital was built it was used as a British Officers Mess for a period before eventually being sold to the Club by the Government. The Penang Golf Club, as it was by then known, was in its new premises for only 3 years before the Japanese invasion and the internment of the, largely European, membership. At the end of WW2, the population returned to a ravaged Georgetown and the members

Food & Beverages
Clubhouse Family Restaurant
Poolside Café
Terrace Restaurant
Terrace Bar
Main Bar

Sports
19 Tennis Courts
Cricket Pitch
2 Badminton Courts
2 Squash Courts
Gymnasium
30-yard Swimming Pool

Miscellaneous
Steam Bath; Hairdressers
TV Room
Billiards Room
Library

Accommodation
The Club can arrange discounted accommodation at the Cititel, a modern, clean, 4-star hotel for approximately RM120 per room. Speak to the General Manager's office for assistance in booking.

The cricket pitch

to a ravaged Club. The Clubhouse had been practically wrecked and the once beautiful grounds had been turned over to the farming of 'ubi kayu'. To make matters worse, the Club had a mere 1,000 Straits dollars in the Bank. After some heroic efforts however, $15,000 were raised from amongst the returning business community and such pre-war members as survived the camps and in 1947 the Club was back in business again, now renamed the Penang Sports Club.

It is the truly excellent sports facilities, the huge space and the lovely green surroundings which make the Penang Sports Club worthy both of mention and of a visit. This efficiently managed and prosperous club ploughs back virtually every penny received from the members into the maintenance of the Clubhouse and grounds or, very creditably, into sponsoring young sports men and women. The swimming pool is new, well maintained and has beautiful Penang Hill as a backdrop. There are 19 immaculate tennis courts, 8 of which are of manicured grass, 2 squash courts and a gymnasium.

Cricket is a passion: there are 7 wickets—each formed of a different type of grass and each chosen for play according to the nature of the weather. Serious cricket. Happily, the old wooden cricket pavilion still survives.

For visitors to the island the Sports Club provides a perfect escape from the noise of the city and an ideal place to spend the

Club grounds

day either lounging by the swimming pool or taking advantage of the fantastic sports facilities. There is room to breathe and to relax here and lots of space for children to run around in safety and with grass underneath their feet. The grounds are well kept, secure and child safe. The food is good, particularly the Asian food and again, particularly if taken on the Terrace.

Although there is no accommodation at the club, they do have a very good corporate deal with a nearby hotel, detailed on page 74. Jalan Utama is, like most of Georgetown, a 25-minute taxi ride from Penang Airport and is a 5-minute ride from the Penang Club, the E&O Hotel and from Gurney Drive. Parking at the club is free and ample.

RECIPROCAL CLUBS

Hong Kong
Hong Kong Football Club
The Kowloon Cricket Club

Thailand
The British Club
The Royal Bangkok Sports Club

Malaysia
Royal Ipoh Club
Royal Selangor Club
Royal Port Dickson Yacht Club

Singapore
Singapore Cricket Club
The Tanglin Club

Australia
The Sandringham Club
The Royal Automobile Club
The Royal South Yarra Lawn Tennis Club

Main entrance

Penang Swimming Club

Old clubhouse with beach and boatyard beyond

The Penang Swimming Club stands roughly equidistant between Georgetown and Batu Feringhi on the northeast coast of Penang. Tanjung Bungah takes its name from the exquisite gardens of the many colonial bungalows built in the area in the early part of the last century, many of which, happily, still survive. The Club lies between the Batu Feringhi Road and the sea, occupying an expansive, 400-yard stretch of the coast. From everywhere are glorious, uninterrupted views across the Straits of Malacca towards Kedah Hill. The location is superb.

The Club was formed in 1903 by a group of European men at a cost of 3,000 Straits Dollars which paid for a Clubhouse

517 Tanjung Bungah
11200 Penang
Malaysia

Tel: +604 890 7370
Fax: +604 890 3271

www.penangswimclub.com
Email: info@penangswimclub.com

Pool with Snake Temple to the left

Pool with new clubhouse to the right

and a diving tower 50 yards out to sea (the skeleton of which still remains). The Clubhouse was extended in 1923 and this lovely, open building still stands at the northern end of the pool. Members pursued all manner of watersports and the Club quickly gained a name for having some of the best fishing in Penang as well as swimming and sailing. Sailing became the big sport in the 1950s and for many years, races were started by a Mary Brown of the Brown Rubber Estate at Glugor, by firing a cannon from the Old Quarterdeck: never before 2 pm however, according to one old member, so as not to interfere with the 'too good to hurry curry'!

Food & Beverages
The Captain's Restaurant
The Captain's Deck
The New Quarter Deck
Snake Temple: seafood and curries
Seafront Café
'Fun' Pub

Sports facilities
Sailing
Angling
Scuba Diving
50-metre Pool
Gymnasium
2 Tennis Courts
2 Squash Courts

Miscellaneous
Boat Berthing
Sauna
Library

Also, in the 1950s came the Emergency with its consequent influx of British and Australian Servicemen to the island. The Club was patronised heavily during this period by RAF and RAAF personnel and very quickly, profits from the bar were double that of the restaurant! The Australian influence continued all the way into the 1980s with the stationing of over 2,000 RAAF personnel and their families on the Island as part of a defence treaty with Malaysia. The married quarters were situated on the slopes above the Club and every day, after school, dozens of mothers would descend with their broods to the Swimming Club to swim and play away the heat of the day: 'blissful years' as described to me by one former Airman, 'we thought we were in heaven'.

The Club's finances are sound and membership is 3,000 and rising. The main building is modern, clean and efficient, and looks down on to the magnificent 50-metre pool. At the far end of the pool is the old clubhouse, perfect for a drink or for lunch and beyond that lie the boat moorings, yard and private beach. The Snake Temple at the south end of the pool serves superb Penang curries. There is good sailing at the Club and visitors can hire boats by the day. There is also good offshore fishing to be had and scuba diving by prior arrangement. The tennis and squash courts are new and in excellent condition. Sadly there is no accommodation and they have no corporate deals with local hotels but the obvious answer of course is to stay at the Penang Club and drive up to the Swimming Club for a sail and for lunch by the sea. The club is 15-minutes by taxi from the centre of Georgetown. There is ample parking.

RECIPROCAL CLUBS

UK
The Carlton Club
Royal Northern and University Club
Royal Scots Club
City University Club

Hong Kong
The Kowloon Cricket Club
Ladies' Recreation Club

Thailand
The British Club

Malaysia
Royal Ipoh Club
Royal Lake Club
Royal Selangor Club
Royal Port Dickson Yacht Club

Singapore
Hollandse Club
Singapore Cricket Club
The Tanglin Club

Australia
The Royal Automobile Club

Taiping New Club

The New Club entrance

Every now and then, in a moment of distraction, it can for some be a soothing diversion to step back briefly from the present into the past and it is for this reason, primarily, that the New Club is in the guide. The New Club is not for adherents to the new. Rather it is for the adventurous, for the nostalgic, for those who have enjoyed the baleful short stories of Somerset Maugham and for those who simply wish to take a fleeting glimpse of their grandfather's or father's lives before flying back to reality. It will be clear already therefore that guacamole and polenta do not

1 Jalan New Club
34007 Taiping
Perak D.R.
West Malaysia

Tel: +605 808 2005
Fax: +605 807 3935

No website.

The dance floor

Swimming pool

figure highly on the menu. Neither do fizzy Italian water nor Pomerol figure on the drinks list. Founded in the early 1880s as a breakaway from the haughty Perak Club which excluded both junior officers and planters, the New Club grew and prospered gradually, becoming, with some justice, the pre-eminent of the two. Then, about 45 years ago, the New Club went into a time warp when the British Army left at the end of the 'Emergency', when both tin and rubber prices went into seemingly terminal decline and when what remained of business in Perak State became centred upon Ipoh, 50 miles further down the road towards Kuala Lumpur. Indeed the same can be said for Taiping itself, a town which had its moment of glory when it was the state capital, which had a brief flirtation with modernity in the 1970s when a few tragic examples of modern architecture were raised, only to fall into neglect after a few years when the town realised that progress was to pass it by. Taiping, as well as its Club, is a time warp. Half shut your eyes and it is full of ghosts.

Taiping means 'Everlasting Peace' in Chinese and was the name given to this little town by one Captain Tristram Speedy of the Indian Army whose soldiers had quelled riots between

Lists of Past Presidents

gangs of rival Chinese miners in the area in the 1860s. The town became the administrative centre for this prosperous tin-mining area and early town planning was guided by Sir Hugh Low and then Frank Swettenham, respectively Resident and acting Resident of Perak in the 1880s. Much of the architecture from this period survives in the form of government offices, schools, barracks, Officers' messes, churches, etc, and these can all be seen when you wander along what the town calls its heritage trail, which is essentially a meander along the seldom visited lanes of the town's colonial past. The New Club lies on this trail on the corner of the Esplanade, equidistant from the former British Officers' Mess, Fort Carnarvon and the Residency. Primarily of wooden construction with double height ceilings, an ante room, a dance floor, a dining room and a bar, it is simple and typical of its place and time. Neither the restaurant nor the bar will detain you for long but the former dance floor will, echoing, as it does, to the chatter of planters' wives now long since retired to Cheltenham or to Tunbridge Wells, and bearing on its walls the names of past Club Presidents, now long dead. So too will the anteroom area which opens on to the verandah with its lazy, soporific views out over a sweltering padang. The library seems to have gone into suspended animation in about 1963, the most recent books being dusty, now largely ant-eaten Hammond Innes novels, their accession numbers carefully recorded inside.

There are 850 members of the New Club and it seems well supported. Those members present at the Club when you visit might appear a little surprised to see you: do not misinterpret this surprise for hostility however, visitors to Taiping are rare but nonetheless

The ante room (above); one of the two chambers (right)

welcome. The staff are helpful, friendly and proud of their club. There are two tennis courts, a squash court, a gymnasium and a billiards room as well as a lovely swimming pool. There are two well-maintained and clean accommodation rooms (chambers) available for the princely sum of RM65 per night.

The one English member I met at the Club was a mildly, but pleasantly eccentric man from Neasden, who had made his fortune writing cowboy books and who had settled for 30 years near Taiping, farming turkeys. His was interesting company and he was largely content with his lot. His only complaint about life in Taiping was that as a foreigner, he could not be granted a gun license which necessitated him having to spear, rather than shoot, the 6–8 foot long monitor lizards which forever tried to eat his turkeys and sometimes, him.

Taiping lies east of the main highway roughly 50 miles both from Penang and from Ipoh. A car is a necessity: hire one either in Georgetown or in Kuala Lumpur.

RECIPROCAL CLUBS

Largely lapsed are the words which spring to mind under this heading, sleepy Taiping being very much of its own time and place. Formal reciprocity is restricted mainly to those in Malaysia: the Penang Club, the Penang Swimming Club, the Penang Sports Club, the Royal Ipoh Club, the Royal Selangor Club and the Royal Port Dickson Yacht Club. Bizarrely, the Hong Kong Football Club is the only foreign Club of note, which still reciprocates. In this instance, this short list is largely academic: visitors to the New Club can buy day membership for RM10 per day.

SINGAPORE

The British Club
Hollandse Club
The Tanglin Club

The Tanglin Club (above); Cavenagh Bridge looking over the UOB Building in the background, Singapore (previous pages)

An Ode to the Tanglin Club

In days of yore, so goes the lore,

They used to dance at Tanglin,

When party girls with winsome curls

From apron strings were danglin',

And mothers proud remarked out loud,

'How nicely Maud is dancing:

With look demure, complexion pure,

She's really quite entrancing.'

RLD Wodehouse, *The Straits and States Annual* 1919

The British Club

The clubhouse

Given that Stamford Raffles established the settlement of Singapore for Great Britain as far back as 1819, it comes as something of a surprise to visitors to learn that The British Club is in fact a fairly new addition to Singapore's role call of Clubs. The reason is that same British Colonial past: it was The Tanglin Club which was for over 100 years effectively The British Club. When in 1963, The Tanglin threw membership open to all races, the queues to join quickly grew to the point where the waiting list extended to several years: not much use to a family in Singapore on a 2 or 3-year posting. There was by then, the mid 1960s, a Swiss Club, a Dutch Club, an American Club and a Japanese Club. Earlier, there had also been a German Club, the Teutonia Club on the site of today's Goodwood Hotel (appropriated by the Singapore Authorities in

73 Bukit Tinggi Road
Singapore 289761

Tel: +65 6467 4311
Fax: +65 6468 6161

www.britichclub.org.sg
Email: enquiries@britishclub.org.sg

Another view of the swimming pool

The swimming pool

WW1 and never returned). A move to start a British Club began therefore in the late 1960s and the Club opened its doors in 1986 being formally opened by Princess Anne one year later.

The Club lies on Bukit Tinggi, the second highest peak in Singapore, on land owned by the nearby Swiss Club. It is the location and layout of the Club which makes it so attractive for the visitor to Singapore. The quiet, 5.4-acre site stretches down the side of a lush, green hill with the separate components of Clubhouse, pool and sports centre being interconnected by winding paths through secondary jungle, the whole creating a kind of mini resort feel. Indeed it is quite possible to spend the entire day there without seeing the children, or indeed the spouse, more than you might wish to! There are over 2,000 members of

Food & Beverages
Mountbatten Room: fine dining
Verandah Terrace: alfresco
Verandah Café: family dining
Windsor Arms: English pub
Racquets Bar: sports complex
Rooftop Bar: views!
Poolside Bar

Sports facilities
4 Squash Courts
4 Tennis Courts

Gymnasium
30-yard Swimming Pool
Children's Pool
Football Pitch
Cricket Pitch

Miscellaneous
Library
Reading Room
Billiards Room
Computer Room
Jacuzzi

whom 50 per cent are British. There are 3 International Schools close by so demand for membership is strong. It is very much a family Club and although ideal for the single visitor to Singapore, it is quite perfect for a family.

The Club is well built and well maintained. The Millennium Sports Complex sited on the lower of the three terraces houses a gymnasium, four squash courts and four tennis courts, all in good repair. The food, of all types, is good. All needs are catered to, from fine dining in the Mountbatten Room through Singapore noodles with the family by the pool, to bangers and mash in the Pub. The Club is very child-friendly and the grounds are safe and secure although there is a perennial problem of thieving monkeys which can sometimes be a nuisance. Whilst it is highly amusing to see a monkey get the fright of his life when the mobile phone he has stolen suddenly rings, it's somehow not quite so funny if it is your own! Particularly if he then drops it into the pool. Discounted golf in Singapore and over the causeway in Malaysia are available if you approach the Club office in advance. There is no accommodation but the Club will offer advice on where to stay at rates discounted for reciprocal members.

The Club is a 20-minute taxi ride from the airport and a 10-minute ride from the shopping area of Orchard Road. The car park is large, free and open to visitors. Security is quite tight: be armed with identification.

RECIPROCAL CLUBS

Canada
The Halifax Club
The Union Club of British Columbia

UK
The Lansdowne Club
The Naval Club
The Travellers Club
Ulster Reform Club
The Western Club

Hong Kong
Hong Kong Cricket Club
Hong Kong Football Club
The Kowloon Cricket Club

Thailand
The British Club
The Capitol Club

Malaysia
Penang Club
Royal Ipoh Club
Royal Selangor Club

Australia
Athenaeum Club
City Tattersalls Club
Huntingdon Club
Queensland Cricketers' Club
The Royal Automobile Club (Sydney)
Tattersall's Club
Victorian Club
The Western Australian Club

Hollandse Club

The new spa

The Hollandse, or Dutch Club, was formed in 1908 by a group of Dutch businessmen, most of whom worked in the Singapore offices of trading companies operating in the Dutch East Indies islands of Java, Sumatra and southern Borneo. The Club was located at Cairnhill Circle until occupation by the Japanese in 1942. Post war, the Club restarted on land bought for them by the Dutch Commerce Bank (precursor to the ABN AMRO now) in Camden Park and a Clubhouse was completed in 1952, since rebuilt. The Club has recently undergone another major refurbishment involving a rebuild of the tennis pavilion and the

22 Camden Park
Singapore 299814

Tel: +65 6464 5225
Fax: +65 6468 6272

www.hollandseclub.org.sg
Email: info@hollandseclub.org.sg

Hollandse Club in Camden Park

The new health club

opening of a state-of-the-art Spa which is to be run by the highly reputable Spa chain, Aspara. Whilst the Dutch Club is in the first rank, it is this Spa which ensures the Club's place in this guide. Housed as it is in a smart new building containing all the necessary components of massage, steambath, nail bars, etc, at rates up to 40 per cent below market, without the queues and centrally located, the Spa is a big draw both to members and visitors alike. There is also a child-minding service (the Puppy Club) which allows mothers actually to get into the Spa and not just dream of it. The food at all of the outlets is good but most interesting is Chan Fu Ji, the Cantonese restaurant opened in 2004 which is ideal for couples. Families would find the Terrace easier, serving as it does both Asian and Western dishes and being only seconds from the swimming pool.

Membership stands at 1,400; 27 per cent of whom are Dutch and 17 per cent of whom are British. 10 other nationalities make

Food & Beverages
Juliana's: Mediterranean and Western food
The Terrace: outdoors, family dining, Asian and Western food
Chan Fu Ji: Cantonese food
Tradewinds Bar
Serambi Bar
Poolside Bar and Café
Sports Pavilion Bar

Club entrance

The swimming pool

up the rest. There is no accommodation but the Club has a corporate deal with a local hotel within walking distance which discounts the rack rate by 40 per cent.

The Club is easy to find, lying near Adam Road just off the Pan Island Expressway. Parking is free and ample. The airport is a 25-minute ride by taxi, Orchard Road is 10 minutes away.

RECIPROCAL CLUBS

UK
The Lansdowne Club
St. James's Club

South Africa
Cape Town Club

Hong Kong
Foreign Correspondents' Club
United Services Recreation Club

Malaysia
Penang Swimming Club
Raintree Club

Singapore
Changi Sailing Club
Singapore Polo Club

Australia
The Royal Automobile Club
Tattersall's Club

Sports facilities
5 Astro Turf Tennis Courts
2 Squash Courts
270sq metre Gymnasium
Bowling Alley
A 30-yard swimming pool

Accommodation
The Club has a deal with the nearby Copthorne Orchid Hotel. Rooms are S$122, a 40-per cent discount to the rack rate. Book through the Club.

Miscellaneous
Child-minding Service
Children's Computer Room
Library
Spa with hot tubs, massage, various aromatherapy treatments, nail therapy, etc, run by Aspara, rates are 40 per cent or so of the commercial, non-Club equivalent.

The Tanglin Club

Main clubhouse and pool

The Tanglin Club is very much one of the Grande Dames of South East Asia. Its excellent location, first-rate facilities and reputation as an elite institution have established it as the Club to belong to in Singapore for well over a century.

The Club was founded in 1865, only 46 years after Stamford Raffles established the settlement of Singapore itself. It was built in the area called Tanglin, a corruption of Tung-Lien meaning Eastern Wood, which hitherto had been turned over to the

5 Stevens Road
Singapore 257814

Tel: +65 6737 6011
Fax: +65 6733 2391

www.tanglinclub.org.sg
Email: tcfoh@tanglin-club.org.sg

Guest room

farming of coffee and spices on just over an acre of land on Arthur Hughes de Wind's Claymore Estate. The first Clubhouse was built at a cost of 5,000 Spanish dollars (as in Shanghai, Spanish Dollars, actually minted in and exported from Mexico, were the common currency of the time). Over the next several decades, the Club prospered in tandem with the economy of the Settlement with both Government and life in general improving when rule passed from Calcutta to London, rule from Calcutta being a hangover from the Honourable East India Company days. When in 1869, the Suez Canal opened cutting the sailing time from London to Singapore from 116 days to 42, a new influx of settlers and investors from Britain arrived and the economy took off. By 1903, the Port of Singapore, by tonnage moved, was the seventh largest in the world.

The Great Depression of 1929 damaged the international trade on which Singapore was so dependent and as Singapore's finances worsened, so did those of the Tanglin Club. The young (and therefore less well paid) stayed away and it became to some, the sort of place where 'one old boffin had his own chair and if anyone sat in it there was hell to pay'. However, a vigorous new committee took over in 1933 giving away, with tremendous foresight, free membership to one hundred new members (carefully handpicked however, for their track record of using that great profit centre of the bar) and the Tanglin's fortunes changed. It became fashionable again and was, in Anthony Hill's words in his 'Diversion in Malaya', 'a cheerful place' and, unlike the Singapore Cricket Club, did not have a 'waiter-please-remove-this-gentleman-he's-been-dead-for-three-days sort of atmosphere'.

Food & Beverages
Churchill Room: fine dining
Foyer Lounge: tea, sandwiches, etc
The Tavern: bar and pub grub
The Wheelhouse: casual restaurant
near the swimming pool

Sports facilities
5 Squash Courts
6 Tennis Courts
30-yard Swimming Pool
Gymnasium

Miscellaneous
Library (10,000 books)
Reading room
Billiards room
Hairdresser
Cybercafé
Children's Library

Accommodation
16 rooms, all en suite with safe, minibar, TV and aircon. S$190 per night.

The Churchill Room

Reinstated in 1946 after the Japanese Occupation during the war, the Club saw a surge in Service membership during the Emergency in Malaya, but for some, it was not developing sufficiently quickly to keep pace with the changing political and social times. Indeed Somerset Maugham, temporarily refused access to the Club in 1959 for not wearing a jacket and tie, surveying the bar said, 'observing these people I am no longer surprised that there is such a scarcity of domestic servants back home in England'. The records do not show what the members thought of him, nevertheless a point was made, not so much about dress but about the need for the Club to adapt to a changing world. This the Club did and gradually it became a shade more relaxed, more child- and family-friendly and membership was eventually opened to all, irrespective of class, colour or creed in the 1960s.

And still the Club absolutely thrives. Membership stands at 6,000 with anything up to a 7-year waiting list. The 51 per cent membership quota system ensures that no one race can dominate and there are now 71 different nationalities on the books.

Whilst still more formal than most (a fact which suits many), the Club is nevertheless welcoming to visitors and to their families. The accommodation is excellent, as are the sports facilities. The Churchill Room is a beautiful dining room with

a well-deserved reputation for very good food. The Tavern Bar is more casual and with its photographs, Regimental plaques and presentation pieces of all kinds forms a fascinating social record of Singapore. The informal Wheelhouse Restaurant by the swimming pool is the perfect place for a family lunch. At the time of writing a major refurbishment is just being finished, including the construction of a brand new sports complex housing tennis and squash courts, lawn bowls, a gymnasium, a spa and a health club. The Tanglin deserves its reputation as one of the world's great Clubs. Book very, very early in advance: it is popular.

The Club is a 25-minute taxi ride from the airport and is 15 minutes from Orchard Road and the CBD.

RECIPROCAL CLUBS

Canada
The Glencoe Club
The National Club
The Union Club of British Columbia
The Vancouver Club

UK
The Army and Navy Club
Athenaeum Club
Caledonian Club
The Carlton Club
The Cavalry and Guards Club
The East India Club
The Hurlingham Club
The Naval Club
Naval and Military Club
The New Cavendish Club
Oriental Club
Oxford and Cambridge Club
The Reform Club
Royal Over-Seas League
Victoria Club

Kenya
Muthaiga Country Club

South Africa
Johannesburg Country Club
Durban Country Club
Inanda Club

Hong Kong
Hong Kong Club
Hong Kong Football Club

Thailand
The British Club
The Royal Bangkok Sports Club

Malaysia
Penang Club
Penang Sports Club
Penang Swimming Club
Royal Ipoh Club
Royal Lake Club
Royal Port Dickson Yacht Club

Australia
The Adelaide Club
The Australian Club
The Brisbane Club
The Commonwealth Club
The Melbourne Club
The Royal Automobile Club (Sydney)
Royal Sydney Yacht Squadron
Tattersall's Club (Brisbane)
Tattersall's Club (Sydney)
United Service Club
The Weld Club
The West Australian Club

New Zealand
Auckland Club
The Christchurch Club
The Dunedin Club
The Northern Club

AUSTRALIA

Painting by Sir Arthur Streeton—property of The Naval and Military Club, Melbourne (above); Melbourne Savage Club (previous pages)

In the 1970s the death of (Australian) Clubs (small republics with their own rules and traditions… governed by an oligarchy) was pronounced. Great social changes appeared to have made them irrelevant… in fact Clubs have resembled alpine flowers on the edge of a precipice… they have survived and flourished despite the bewildering change (of) society.

From 'About the Club', *The Australian*, Melbourne

The Australian Club

William Street entrance

By the 1870s there were already four established Clubs in Melbourne. No Clubs existed however in the western, commercial end of the city so in 1878, a group of merchants, businessmen and farmers led by a Scot named James MacBain formed the Australian Club in William Street, within sight of the big mercantile and shipping houses, the Wool Exchange and the warehouses and wharves on the Yarra River. The Club still retains its trading roots and remains the premier business Club in Melbourne.

The Clubhouse is a magnificent, 5-storey Victorian building which stands in a very prominent position at the junction of William Street and Little Collins Street, no more than 500 yards from the River. For the visitor either on business or on holiday,

110 William Street
Melbourne
Victoria 3000
Australia

Tel: +61 3 9672 1700
Fax: +61 3 9600 0656

www.theaustralianclub.com.au
(Reciprocal password needed from the Club)
Email: gm@theaustralianclub.com.au

the location is quite perfect. No expense was spared in the construction of the Club and this fact becomes immediately apparent on walking into the hall: the intricate mosaic floor is so beautiful you almost feel the need to tread softly as you cross the hall past the grand central staircase, a staircase seemingly unsupported but in fact held aloft by being cantilevered into the walls. Don't hold your breath: almost every room in this Club has something about it which is extraordinary and although the feel is very much mahogany and old leather (it is still a men's Club with some restrictions on women), many rooms are brightened by the addition over the years of some beautiful paintings (some of the best painted by women!).

The main dining room is on the ground floor. It is a huge and grand room with a beautiful and huge chandelier bought from a Maharaja's Palace in 1978 to commemorate the Club's centenary. At the back of the hall is the Members' Bar, a very convivial place housing all sorts of interesting Club memorabilia including a 20-lb pair of 1832 wine coolers and a silver urn containing the ashes of Gurness Lane, a Melbourne Cup winner which helped a few members win a quid or two one memorable year!

The Strangers' Room and the Long Room are two private bars where members take male guests for pre-lunch drinks, the Members' Bar being members only until 1430. It is the first floor which is very much the area for reciprocal members: do not be put off by any perceived 'them and us' in this regard however, most of the nicest rooms are here on the 1st floor beginning with the Gould Lounge where men and women can have drinks before lunch whilst admiring some of the light, pretty and breezy

Food & Beverages
Presidents' Dining Room
Members' Bar (after 1430hrs)
Gould Lounge: drinks
Strangers' Room: drinks
Long Room: drinks

Miscellaneous
Morning Room: newspapers and coffee
Billiards Room
Library

Accommodation
19 rooms, all en suite, beginning at Aus$105 per room.

paintings of famed local artist, Ellis Rowan. All three meals are served in the Presidents' Dining Room which is a lovely room and less austere than the Members' Dining Room. There are several other interesting rooms to visit on the first floor including the Niall Room which houses several valuable paintings of mammals and birds by John Gould, the Dominoes Room which contains a somewhat haunting self portrait by Charles Wheeler and also the Ellis Rowan Room which contains 13 beautiful murals of native flowers painted by Ellis Rowan in 1893 (amazingly, these were varnished over in the 1930s having been deemed to be too bright for a men's Club. They were brilliantly restored in the 1980s using 16,000 balls of cotton wool). There is a three-table Billiards Room on the mezzanine floor and whether a player or not, do not forget to take a peak inside at the scarily huge, wall-mounted head of a 10ft, 371-lb swordfish which took one FN Grimwade a full 95 minutes to land in 1935.

Whilst welcoming to reciprocal members, The Australian Club is still a somewhat private affair, hence the ground floor restrictions on non-members of both sexes. Hence also the lack of photographs: whilst the Club staff were very happy to show me around, they were not too happy to see a camera. Put these 'isms' aside though: it is a great Club in a convenient spot in town which has very good accommodation at good rates and which has a nice, comfortable feel about it.

RECIPROCAL CLUBS

Canada
The University Club of Toronto
The Union Club of British Columbia
The Vancouver Club

UK
The Carlton Club
City University Club
The East India Club
The Lansdowne Club
The Naval and Military Club
The New Club Edinburgh
Oriental Club
Oxford and Cambridge Club
The Travellers Club
The Western Club

South Africa
The Kimberley Club
The Rand Club

Hong Kong
The Hong Kong Club

Singapore
The Tanglin Club

Australia
The Adelaide Club
The Australian Club (Sydney)
Queensland Club
Union Club (Sydney)
The Weld Club

New Zealand
Auckland Club
The Christchurch Club
The Dunedin Club
The Northern Club
The Wellington Club

Melbourne Savage Club

Long Room

By the mid to late 1800s, Clubs in London which catered to the Arts had become firmly established with the Athenaeum and the Garrick very much to the fore. For some young writers and artists however, these Clubs had become rather too established and a feeling grew within younger literary circles that the atmosphere of some of the Arts Clubs had become altogether too rarified. Indeed membership of the Royal Academy was a prerequisite for an artist even to be considered for membership of the Athenaeum. Kipling gave fluent voice to these growing concerns, once saying that to visit the Athenaeum was to 'visit the Cathedral between services'.

12 Bank Place
Melbourne
Victoria 3000
Australia

Tel: +61 3 9670 0644
Fax: +61 3 9600 1176

www.melbournesavageclub.com
Email: melbsavage@bigpond.com

The Bank Place entrance

Smoking Room stage, scene of countless smoke nights or musical evenings

The Earl of Birkenhead then gave not voice but inadvertent action as it were to this mood, by regularly using the Athenaeum as a convenience, on the way to his office each day, exclaiming 'Great God! Do you mean to tell me this place is a Club?' when at last asked by the Secretary to explain himself. Against this background of perceived stuffiness, some of the more anarchic writers of the day sought to found a home for the 'unwashed and filthy fingered literati'. Discussing a name for the Club at the inaugural meeting of this new home, the names 'Shakespeare' and 'Johnson' were rejected as being too pretentious for inclusion, instead the founders went for the name 'Savage', Richard Savage being a poor, minor and illegitimate poet whose circumstances it was felt, were apt.

The Melbourne Savage Club was Australia's answer to this same, if later felt feeling and was formed in 1894 growing out of the musical appreciation societies of the 1880s. From the outset,

Food & Beverages
Third World Bar
Main Dining Room
Private Dining Room
Yorrick Basement Tavern

Accommodation
18 Bank Place apartments for both short and long stays.
Call +613 9604 4321 or ask the Savage Club Secretary for help.

Long Room

Various club artefacts including part of the Wisdom Collection from Papua New Guinea and Yorrick; the skull from the Yorrick Club

music was at the heart of the Club. A full concert Vogel grand piano was bought in 1897 which formed the heart of the quartets playing to the members at the many, and famous 'Smoke Nights' held at the Club: evenings of concerts or sometimes plays to which an invitation was highly prized. The conductor Alberto Zelman was an early member and the Club owns his silver mounted baton which was carved from a branch of the first British oak tree planted in Australia by Governor Arthur Phillip in 1778. Artists Sir Arthur Streeton, Sir John Longstaff and acclaimed caricaturist David Low were also early members of the Club and many of their valuable works now adorn the walls.

In the early 1900s, the Club's membership became more diverse to include barristers, businessmen and soldiers, one of these being General AE Wisdom who became the first administrator of Papua New Guinea (PNG) and whose collection of extraordinary 'native' artefacts of spears, shields and the like now lie in, and indeed all over, the Club.

The building owned and occupied by the Club is a handsome, three-storey Victorian town house in the very smart Bank Place. It was built in 1884 as the private home of local worthy landowner and later statesman, Sir Rupert Clarke, who sold it in 1923 to the Savage Club. The house is quite lovely. It is a solidly built, imposing building with a well-maintained exterior which manages to sit very happily amongst the trendy Bank Place wine bars. As you go through the door however, you enter another world. The ground floor consists almost entirely of

Dining room complete with working Punkahs

the Smoking Room (think anteroom) which has an open fire at each end, a stage in the middle, comfortable leather chairs and sofas in abundance and walls which groan under the weight of the Wisdom PNG collection and also of caricatures and paintings by former members including the stunning 'Warrandyke' by the acclaimed Penleigh Boyd.

On the first floor are a very grand billiard room, the much-admired Long Room, essentially a portrait gallery and venue for art exhibitions and the private dining room where ladies are entertained to lunch. Also on the first floor is the much-used Third World Bar with again, paintings, caricatures and extraordinary artefacts sufficient to keep a visitor fascinated for hours. The dining room, complete with working punkahs is on the second floor. It has a reputation for very good food and for even better wine.

Former premier Sir Robert Menzies was President of the Club from 1947 until 1962. The polite intolerance of pomposity, artistic or otherwise, which formed part of the Club's founding character, indeed raison d'etre, was illustrated quite perfectly by Menzies when a new Secretary began work in 1930. His name was St John Scott-Scott. 'Ah Scott,' said Menzies, 'pleased to meet you. Let me buy you a drink.' 'Actually, the name is Scott-Scott, Thank you.' 'Really?' said Menzies, 'Then let me buy you two.' And then years later, when an exasperated waiter hurled a glass of whisky at the wall in the Smoking Room exclaiming, 'I think this damned Club is a garbage dump of a Club,' he was sacked for wasting good whisky, not for telling what the members happily agreed was the truth! (It is not the truth, but how refreshingly unpompous!)

The Savage is the last of the Bohemian Arts Clubs in Melbourne having taken over the other survivor, the Yorrick, in 1966. (Yes, there is a skull, sent from Egypt by Sir Stanley

The Third World Bar

Argyle in 1915. Housed on the landing—it grins at you as you walk up to the bar). It is a mildly but wonderfully anachronistic Club, both in character and in content and in this increasingly authoritarian and conformist world in which we live, one wonders whether such an idiosyncratic gathering of 550 friends will escape a visit from some future Thought and Behaviour Directorate. True, the restrictions on ladies (not before 4.30 pm except in the Private Dining Room) may offend some. Try to put up with it here though: the Savage is a fascinating, warm, comfortable refuge, full of history, full of art and full of conviviality and a gin in the Third World Bar, lunch under the punkahs and a gaze at the art collection are a true privilege for the visitor. Don't miss this Club.

Accommodation is available next door at 18 Bank Place which is not part of the Club itself, but which is a neat, discrete set of apartments with which the Club has negotiated very good rates.

RECIPROCAL CLUBS

Canada
The Halifax Club
Mount Stephen Club
The Ontario Club
The Union Club of British Columbia

UK
Bucks Club
City University Club
Oxford and Cambridge Club
St. James's Club
The Travellers Club
Ulster Reform Club
The Western Club

Thailand
The British Club

Singapore
Singapore Cricket Club

Australia
The Brisbane Club
The Geelong Club
Union Club (Sydney)
Union, University and Schools' Club of Sydney
The Western Australian Club

New Zealand
Hawkes Bay Club
The Northern Club

The Naval and Military Club

Guest Room

Established in 1881 as the PipeClay Club by Officers of the Victoria Defence Forces in rooms in the Earl of Zetland hotel on Swanston Street, The Naval and Military Club as it was eventually to be renamed, very quickly became the natural home for both Regular and Reserve Officers stationed in and around Melbourne. This grand old Club has an illustrious history and over the decades many of the great and the good of Australia's Armed Forces have been members, including such figures as the statesman-like WW1 General Sir John Monash, General Sir Thomas Blamey who became Australia's only Field Marshall being awarded his baton whilst on his deathbed and Air Marshall Sir Richard Williams, the 'Father' of the Royal

27 Little Collins Street
Melbourne
Victoria 3000
Australia

Tel: +61 3 9650 4741
Fax: +61 3 9650 6529

www.nmclub.com.au
Email: enquiries@nmclub.com.au

Dining room (right); entrance hall (facing page)

The Terrace Garden

Australian Air Force. The Club is rightly proud of the fact that such great men belonged and also of the fact that it counts 7 VCs amongst former members. The Prince of Wales and the Duke of Edinburgh are both current Life Members, as was one of the very best soldiers of them all: General Bill Slim.

The great surge in post WW2 membership prompted a move out of the lovely, but cramped home in Alfred Place which the Club had occupied since 1919, and into a purpose built new home in Little Collins Street. Then a state-of-the-art 1960's building, it now suffers from some of the architectural challenges associated with many buildings of that period, in that they appear often not so much to weather as to tire, and it would be disingenuous to

Food & Beverages
Dining (Streeton) Room
Terrace Garden
2 Bars

Sports facilities
Gymnasium
2 Squash Courts

Accommodation
18 en suite recently refurbished rooms with TV, internet access, minibar and safe beginning at Aus$125 per room.

Miscellaneous
Billiard Room
Library
Laundry and Dry Dleaning

Accommodation rooms (above and right)

argue that there is much external 'wow' factor. That said, the Club Secretary and Committee, fully aware of this fact, are striving with some success to improve the external appearance and the plans for further improvements are impressive.

It is when you enter the Club and see the combination of the old and the new which is on offer that the reason for the Club's inclusion in this guide becomes clear. In order both to attract younger members and to remain competitive, an extensive renovation program has been underway for some years now and all 18 en suite bedrooms have been refurbished to a very high standard offering 4- to 5-star accommodation at 2- to 3-star prices. And to cater for less formal dining a pretty and modern terrace garden, designed by a respected Melbourne landscape gardener has been added, which provides a bright and airy alternative to the main dining room for casual lunches and suppers. Then, to the rear of the Club, a brand new, immaculate gymnasium complete with two squash courts has been built, all accessed by clever internal routing which precludes the need to step over a sleeping General's legs in order to take that quick, lunch hour workout. All this modernisation has taken time and is as yet not 100 per cent complete but it is close—and most certainly worth it. The more traditional and yet to be

refurbished side of the Club includes a small but interesting library, a comfortable anteroom with bar and the Streeton Room, the main dining room which houses a tremendous and valuable collection of paintings by the WW1 Official War Artist Sir Arthur Streeton, which he donated to the Club. The food in the Dining Room is very good indeed and the wine list, as with so many Australian Clubs, is excellent.

In sum, The Naval and Military is an excellent little Club whose management are responding to the demands of a newer, younger membership with a carefully thought through program of refurbishment, which although not yet complete, is progressing well. To the reciprocating visitor it offers excellent accommodation, a home from home with a comfortable 'clubby' feel, great value without compromising quality and a superb location right on the edge of the CBD. As with most of the city centre, the Club lies about 30 minutes by taxi from the Airport. There is ample public parking a little further down Little Collins Street.

RECIPROCAL CLUBS

Canada
Mount Stephen Club
The Royal Canadian Military Institute
The Union Club of British Columbia
The National Liberal Club (Toronto)

UK
The Army and Navy Club
The Carlton Club
City University Club
The Naval and Military Club
The Naval Club
The Norfolk Club
Royal Air Force Club
Royal Naval Club and Royal Albert Yacht Club
Royal Scots Club
The Western Club

Hong Kong
Hong Kong Cricket Club
The Kowloon Cricket Club
Royal Hong Kong Yacht Club
United Services Recreation Club

Thailand
The British Club

Malaysia
Penang Club
Royal Ipoh Club
Royal Lake Club

Australia
The Brisbane Club
Brisbane Polo Club
The Canberra Club
The Royal Automobile Club
Union, University and Schools' Club of Sydney
United Service Club
The Western Australia Club

New Zealand
Auckland Club
The Christchurch Club
The Wellington Club

Dining room (right); ante room(far right)

The Naval, Military and Air Force Club

The clubhouse (above); the club hall (facing page)

Adelaide's Naval and Military Club was founded in 1879 as the 'Militia Officers' Club of South Australia' by one Colonel Francis Downes, Commandant of the South Australia Militia Forces (whose first given name, somewhat confusingly, was Major). After a series of different homes, the Club moved into its current building in 1957. Built in the 1870s for local pastoralist John Rounsevell, it makes for the perfect town Clubhouse in that it is the size, shape and configuration of what it was designed to be: a large, family home. It is a lovely building, solidly constructed of local bluestone and looks for all the world like it has been plucked off the streets of Harrogate or of Edinburgh and shipped to the other end of

573/6
111 Hutt Street
Adelaide
South Australia 5000

Tel: +61 8 8223 2422
Fax: +61 8 8232 3082

www.navmil.org
Email: admin@navmil.org

Food & Beverages
Main Dining Room
Club Bar: also light lunches
Guests' Breakfast Room

Miscellaneous
Billiards Room
Squash Court
Library
Card Room

Accommodation
5 rooms, all en suite beginning at
Aus$125 per night.

Dining room (above); the bar (right)

the earth. Inside, it is just as 'Harrogate': perfectly proportioned rooms with big tall ceilings, picture rails, mighty architraves and substantial marble fireplaces everywhere which happily are in daily use in the cold weather.

The centre of the Club is the bar, a long and large room, loosely divided into three sections, the walls of which groan under the weight of fascinating militaria, much of which, unsurprisingly, is related to the Japanese surrender in WW2. It is a convivial, if slightly musty bar which seems well patronized and which also serves good light lunches. The main dining room is a grand, mahogany tabled room, more suited perhaps to General Fireblast than to his daughters but is nevertheless, no less comfortable for that. The food is substantial, traditional and rather good.

There are four private rooms: Imperial, Air Force, Downes and Gallipoli, which all lie on the ground floor and which double up as quiet corners in which to read.

On the first floor is a very good library, a pretty little card room which often resonates to the clack clack clack of busily moving Mahjong tiles, and also the five accommodation rooms. These are large, clean, en suite and comfortable but not modernised for some years: fear not—they are absolutely fine—just don't expect matching furniture or Floris bathsoaps.

Outside and off to one side is a small but nice little garden, behind which is the terrace off the main dining room: a great spot for lunch on a warm day. There is a squash court to the rear of the Club and for the less athletic, a billiards room to the rear of the bar.

The Naval, Military and Air Force Club is a good Club: warm, convivial and housed in a beautiful building. It also has a great Service history as evidenced by the 126 members who served in WW1 and the 234 who served in WW2, and also by the tremendous and valuable collection of medals mounted in the

The medal collection in the bar (above); the library (right)

bar (so valuable in fact that they were stolen in 1986 but quickly recovered after some very clever detective work). A little worn around the edges and a little too unmodernised for some it may be: still, it is a comfortable and grand old lady and it constitutes an excellent home from home for a visit to Adelaide and, very happily, an excellent jumping off point for wine tours along the Barrosa Valley (reds) which lies less than one hour up the road and along the Southern Vales (whites) which lie less than 45 minutes from the Club.

The Club lies 15 minutes by taxi from the Airport and is only a five-minute walk from Victoria Square. There is ample parking.

RECIPROCAL CLUBS

Canada
Rideau Club
The Royal Canadian Military Institute
The Union Club of British Columbia

UK
The Army and Navy Club
The Cavalry and Guards Club
The East India Club
The Naval and Military Club
The Naval Club
The New Club Edinburgh
Phyllis Court Club
Royal Air Force Club
Royal Scots Club
Ulster Reform Club
The Western Club

Hong Kong
Hong Kong Football Club
The Kowloon Cricket Club
United Services Recreation Club

Thailand
The British Club

Malaysia
Penang Club
Royal Selangor Club
Royal Ipoh Club

Australia
The Brisbane Club
The Commonwealth Club
Melbourne Savage Club
The Naval and Military Club
The Royal Automobile Club
United Service Club
The Western Australia Club

New Zealand
The Dunedin Club
Hawkes Bay Club
The Northern Club

The terrace

The Royal Automobile Club of Australia

The clubhouse

The RACA came into being as a result of a mild altercation between Sydney motoring pioneer, Harrie Skinner, and the local Transit Department (think Transport Police) who one day in 1903 'nicked' him for leaving his vehicle unattended. No, parking restrictions had not yet been invented, nor had car bombs: officialdom was 'worried it might start on its own initiative and cause serious damage'. Harrie Skinner must have

89 Macquarie Street
Sydney
New South Wales 2000
Australia

Tel: +61 2 8273 2300
Fax: +61 2 0273 2301

www.raca.com.au
Email: raca@raca.com.au

The clubhouse entrance

Reading room

understood the official mind well because shortly afterwards, with some friends he formed a 'protection association' which a little later became the RACA.

The Club acquired the Macquarie Street site in 1922 commissioning local architects HE Ross and HR Rowe to design the building, which was completed in 1928 to great acclaim. Solid, grand, tall ceilings and intricate plasterwork, it is a lovely building, spoilt only by the Club's next brush with officialdom when the town engineers built an expressway, an astonishing 6 feet from the right hand wall of the Club. That piece of brutal town planning apart, the location of the RACA is superb, which is one of the main reasons for the Club's inclusion in the guide. It lies 'Harbourside', a short walk from the Opera House, the Rocks, the Botanic Gardens, the Harbour Bridge and from Circular Quay: for the visitor to Sydney it would be difficult to find anywhere more convenient.

Food & Beverages
Members Bar (Victoria Room)
Main Dining Room (Harbour Room)
Imperial Service Club Room and Bar

Sports facilities
Gymnasium

Miscellaneous
Sauna and Steam Room
Massage
Billiards Room
Reading Room

Accommodation
29 en suite rooms each with TV and other conveniences, overlooking the harbour with double rooms beginning at Aus$195.

Victoria Room and Members Bar

The Club merged with the Imperial Services Club (ISC) in 1986, after the ISC found themselves on the wrong side of a badly drafted rent agreement, and to the RACA's credit they have indeed more merged than taken over and the ISC lives on through it's own Lounge and Bar on the 3rd floor and their Services element remains quite strong.

The most impressive room in this grand old building is the Victoria Room on the ground floor which houses the Members bar and which also serves as an anteroom. The most striking feature here is the huge glass ceiling light or cupola which allows natural light to flood into what otherwise could be a gloomily lit room. Also on the ground floor is a small but efficient business centre with internet access. The Reading Room is on the 3rd floor and is a comfortable, quiet retreat in which to read the papers or to write letters. The main dining room, the Harbour Room, is on the 6th floor and it does indeed have some splendid views of the harbour (from the right table!). Perhaps the most beautiful room in the building is the Macquarie Room, now a private dining room. It was at one time THE dining room: pity it lost its job—it is a beautiful room.

There is a first rate gymnasium in the basement and also a sauna, steam room and massage room.

The Club has 29 accommodation rooms of varying grades and stages of modernisation: all however are perfectly comfortable and clean and offer good value. The Club lies 25 minutes in a taxi from the airport and a couple of minutes' walk from Circular Quay train station. There is parking for 50 cars.

The Macquarie Room

RECIPROCAL CLUBS

Canada
The Halifax Club
The National Club
The Royal Canadian Military Institute
The Union Club of British Columbia
The Vancouver Club

UK
Bath and Country Club
The Naval and Military Club
The Naval Club
The Nottingham Club
Royal Air Force Club
The Royal Automobile Club
Royal Northern and University Club
The Royal Scots Club
Ulster Reform Club
The Western Club

Kenya
Muthaiga Country Club
Nairobi Gymkhana Club

South Africa
Cape Town Club
Durban Club
Johannesburg Country Club
Victoria Country Club

Hong Kong
Hong Kong Cricket Club
Hong Kong Football Club
The Kowloon Cricket Club
Ladies' Recreation Club
United Services Recreation Club

Thailand
The British Club

Malaysia
Penang Club
Penang Swimming Club
Royal Ipoh Club
Royal Selangor Club

Singapore
The British Club
Hollandse Club
Singapore Cricket Club

Australia
Athenaeum Club
The Canberra Club
The Naval and Military Club
The Naval, Military and Air Force Club of Australia
United Service Club
The Western Australia Club

New Zealand
Auckland Club
The Canterbury Club
The Christchurch Club
The Dunedin Club
The Northern Club

Listed telephone kiosks

Tattersall's Club

Club from Adelaide Street

'Tatts', as it is popularly known, was founded in 1865 for 'gentlemen of the turf' and is still very much part of the Brisbane and indeed the Queensland establishment. The Club moved to its present Queen Street location in 1926 into a handsome, purpose built, Art Deco masterpiece designed by noted local architect Thomas Ramsey Hall, Hall being chosen to build the new Club because of the acclamation he received for his designs for the City Hall, the Criterion and Carlton hotels. Acutely aware of the Brisbane's climatic problems, Hall was also a master of the art of designing buildings using marble and stone to create cool, spacious interiors and he used this skill to great effect

215 Queen Street
Brisbane
Queensland 4000
Australia

Tel: +61 7 3331 8888
Fax: +61 7 3221 3913

www.tattersallsclub.com
Email: administration@
tattersallsclub.com

Healy (Mixed) Dining Room

Main dining room

at 215 Queens Street. The Club was sympathetically extended and refurbished in 1997 and there exists now a happy blend between the old and the new which works very well indeed and which seems to have satisfied the 5,400 members.

Located in the heart of the CBD, Tatts occupies floors 2 to 6 of the building, the ground floor being a smart shopping mall let to high quality shops from which the Club derives a healthy rental income. In common with some other Australian Clubs, Tatts still maintains some restrictions on the Club's use by women. These restrictions are not too onerous however and will perhaps be overlooked by most because of the Club's excellent facilities.

Food & Beverages
Main Dining Room (Men only)
Healy Room (Mixed Dining)
Needham Room (Private Dining)
Members Bar

Sports facilities
25-meter Indoor Swimming Pool
Gymnasium

Miscellaneous
Library
Barber
Sports Massage
Billiards Room

Art deco mirrors and Queensland Industry Painting in the main dining room

Accommodation
18 en suite rooms each with TV, fridge and minibar beginning at Aus$150 per room per night.

Members Bar (above); Tattersall's club crest (facing page)

Access is via a discretely guarded lift in the mall. On the 2nd floor, probably the most powerful room is the Members Bar, a huge, splendid, double height room with maple-panelled walls with a beautiful neo-classical ceiling by Brisbane craftsman W White. Now a comfortable and relaxed bar, it was to some, in earlier times, the Monday morning scene of a painful settling of wagers post the Saturday races, and the elbow-worn tables over which the business was conducted remain, as do the original punkahs which cooled the brows of disappointed punters as they sipped away their sorrows at the bar.

The main dining room (men only) is a quite stunning example of Art Deco interior design. Completed in 1939, the walls are constructed of Queensland marble and are hung with 6 huge Art Deco mirrors and with paintings of Queensland industry by celebrated local artists. The mixed dining room is the Healy Room which is bright, modern and fairly relaxed and which houses a collection of modern works of art purchased locally by the Club in order to encourage local artists. The food throughout is very good.

The Club has an excellent and well looked after library of 5,000 books, a modern gymnasium and on the 6th floor a 25-metre pool.

Swimming pool on the 6th floor

The accommodation is first rate with 18 five-star en suite rooms located on the 3rd and 4th floors. Occupancy rates are 70 per cent so plan well in advance, particularly if you want to stay during one of the four, hugely popular Tattersall's Race Meetings which the Club runs at Eagle Farm each year.

In sum Tatts is a smart, functional, well-run and well-located Club with an air of no-nonsense efficiency, and which also offers very good value: most definitely 1st Eleven.

RECIPROCAL CLUBS

Canada
The Albany Club
Hamilton Club
Royal Canadian Yacht Club
The Union Club of British Columbia

UK
Caledonian Club
City University Club
The East India Club
The Royal Over-Seas League

Hong Kong
The Kowloon Cricket Club

Thailand
The Royal Bangkok Sports Club

Malaysia
Royal Lake Club

Singapore
The Tanglin Club

Australia
Tattersall's Club (Sydney)
The Royal Automobile Club (Sydney)
The Royal Automobile Club (Melbourne)
The Western Australia Club

New Zealand
Auckland Club
The Dunedin Club

Accommodation floor lobby

United Service Club

The Green House

Of all the many delightful Clubs in this guide, the United Service Club in Brisbane, Queensland, (USC) perhaps best displays that quality so unique to Clubs and so desirable and reassuring to the heavily travelled, of comfortable familiarity unspoilt by predictability or sameness. To wander through this Club, certainly for visitors of British stock, is as to wander through the house of an old friend who has moved to the far side of the world: you know largely what you will find and generally where you will find it—but every room and every object comes with its distinct local identity and form and is of course all the more interesting and exciting for that. The USC somehow contrives successfully to combine a distinctly Australian, more, Queensland identity with a flavour akin to the historical fact of national roots once so deep

183 Wickham Terrace
Brisbane
Queensland 4000
Australia

Tel: +61 7 3831 4433
Fax: +61 7 3832 6307

www.unitedserviceclub.com.au
Email: enquiries@unitedserviceclub.com.au

The hall

into Britain as to lead former Prime Minister Sir Robert Menzies to describe Australia as 'British to the bootstraps'. Again, for the British, in few places will the words kith and kin strike a stronger chord than in the USC and indeed, in Brisbane itself.

This gem of a Club began life in 1892 and was formed by Officers of the Queensland Defence Force, the main driver being Maj Gen John Owen, Commandant of that Force and an Officer who had earlier gained recognition for his part in the defeat of King Cetewayo at the Battle of Ulundi in the Zulu War of 1879. The record of service of former members is second to none: 22 of the 350 members were killed in WW1 and in a survey conducted some years later it was found that a full 20 per cent of the 388

Food & Beverages
Main Dining Room
Servery Bar
Military Bar

Accommodation
14 en suite rooms each with aircon, minibar, TV and radio.
Laundry service available.

Inner hall

*One of the stained glass windows (left);
the dining room (facing page)*

members were holders of either the Distinguished Service Order or the Military Cross, a truly extraordinary proportion. The generosity of spirit concomitant with such service shines through repeatedly in the Club's records which show a huge number of accounts being written off when members died, the Club not wishing too add financial stress to the widow's grief. And it came as no surprise to learn that the Club was sending food parcels throughout WW2 to its sister Club in London, The Army and Navy, only ending such kindness when wartime rationing finally ended in 1950. This spirit extended as far as the 'enemy' too: earlier the Club had entertained to dinner Count Felix von Luckner, former Captain of the WW1 German ship 'Zee Teurfel' whose party trick it subsequently transpired, was to tear his host city's telephone directory in half with his bare hands. He managed Brisbane, with its population in the hundreds of thousands quite comfortably apparently, so too Melbourne, but was in the end defeated, by the seven figures of Sydney.

This warm and friendly Club moved to Wickham Terrace in 1947 to an adjoining pair of beautiful buildings, the first, Montpelier, a handsome Edwardian house of redbrown brick, the second, the Green House, a classic and perfectly beautiful 'Queenslander' complete with textbook 'VJs', (vertical joints) which arouse visiting architects into a highly excited state. Both

houses are lovely, particularly the Green House which continues to draw the attentions of rich businessmen looking for the perfect townhouse. Perhaps not surprisingly the internal layout and use of rooms is similar to that of a Mess. There is a Servery Bar, more of an anteroom really where light lunches and coffee are served and where newspapers are placed. Alongside this lies the Military Bar which is bright, comfortable and cosy, and which comes with an interesting collection of Regimental plaques and prints, and from where there is access to the verandah. There a wide and bright lobby area where tea is sometimes served and which serves as a useful waiting area and beyond that lies the main dining room, a lovely, perfectly proportioned room with original and illuminated stained glass windows and whose walls are hung with one or two lovely paintings, notably an oil of the magnificent jacarandas to the rear of the Club. The wine list is excellent and so is the food: dinner at the USC is a real pleasure. To the front of the Club lies a verandah which runs the length of both buildings, to sit and have an early evening drink is a joy, soft illumination being provided by the port and starboard navigation lights of HMAS Sydney which famously destroyed the German Raider 'Emden' at Cocos Island in 1914.

Maintenance standards and decoration everywhere are excellent. There are paintings and military paraphernalia enough both to satisfy interest and to make plain the Clubs lineage but not so much as to turn it into a museum nor to dim the natural brightness of the rooms. Pride of place above the fire in the anteroom is given to a hugely melancholic, beautiful original entitled 'Fallen Infantryman' by George Washington Lambert, the official war artist to the 1st Battalion AIF in WW1.

Entrance (left); the Military Bar (facing page)

There are 14 accommodation rooms in the Club which are all sizeable, clean, comfortable, and offer extremely good value.

Perhaps the overriding of all the good 'feels' about this bright, cheerful, very well-run and efficient Club is one of friendly, stress-free calm, a state achieved largely thanks to good management and seemingly very happy staff, all of whom appear genuinely committed to the Club and who go about their business with a purposeful air. What a happy state! And what a tremendous Club.

Wickham Terrace lies on the edge of the CBD no more than a five-minute walk from the city centre and from the Central Station and no more than 20 minutes by taxi from the Airport. There is parking for 140 cars.

RECIPROCAL CLUBS

Canada
Mount Stephen Club
The Royal Canadian Military Institute
The Union Club of British Columbia

UK
The Army and Navy Club
The Naval and Military Club
The Naval Club
Oxford and Cambridge Club
Royal Air Force Club
Royal Scots Club
The Western Club

Hong Kong
Foreign Correspondents' Club
The Kowloon Cricket Club
United Services Recreation Club

Thailand
The British Club

Malaysia
Penang Club

Singapore
The Tanglin Club

Australia
The Commonwealth Club
The Naval and Military Club
The Royal Automobile Club
Union, University and Schools' Club of Sydney
The Western Australian Club

New Zealand
The Christchurch Club
Hawkes Bay Club
The Wellington Club

NEW ZEALAND

The Dunedin Club (above); The Virginia creeper-filled façade of the Northern Club (previous pages)

The Siren Song of the South Sea Islands...
when it sounds with musical softness
through the harsh discords of a disordered
world. They seem a refuge of romance,
those islands with their lagoons and flowers
and palm trees and splendid, tropical skies.

Louise Maunsell Field, *New York Times* 1921

The Christchurch Club

Club front from Worcester Street

In a country where one is almost spoilt for choice for great Clubs to stay from Auckland in the north all the way to Dunedin in the south, the Christchurch Club stands out as somewhere special. In recent years this Club has had much care and attention lavished upon it by both a proactive management and by an interested and attentive committee and in all of its facets, it most certainly shows.

A town Club it may be now but its roots are in the country. In the year the Club was founded, 1856, Canterbury's was largely a rural economy, indeed the 5,350 Europeans in the province were outnumbered nearly 40·1 by the 220,000 sheep. The Club was

154 Worcester Street
PO Box 55
Christchurch
New Zealand

Tel: +64 3 366 9461
Fax: +64 3 366 9460

www.christchurchclub.co.nz
Email: cyndy@xtra.co.nz

The courtyard

Ante room

formed by 12 out of town graziers or 'runholders', each of whom farmed a (quite astonishing) average of 35,000 acres at a distance of anything up to 100 miles from Christchurch and who therefore needed a place to stay when they came into town for the farm auctions. With a reputation built upon his designs for Canterbury University and for the Provincial Government Offices, celebrated local architect Benjamin Mountfort was chosen to design the Clubhouse and he drew up plans for an Italianate villa with airy, spacious rooms and an open courtyard, a style which would, it was felt, appeal to the rural members.

Food & Beverages
Dining Room
The Buttery
The Orangery
Members' Bar

Accommodation
7 double rooms, all en suite and with minibars, coffee and tea beginning at NZ$130 per room.

Miscellaneous
Laundry Service
Business Centre

Ladies' Drawing Room

The Buttery

The care and maintenance of Mountfort's work has been overseen by Sir Miles Warren, another Canterbury based architect who has won international acclaim for his (primarily) modernist work and whose skill, complemented by the taste of a highly active women's committee, is evident throughout this Category 1 Heritage Building, from the practical in the external paintwork through to the luxurious in the internal fabrics and furnishings.

The Club occupies a corner plot where Worcester Street meets Latimer Square behind trees planted when the Club itself was built. The main Worcester Street entrance is no longer used and access is via a pretty Courtyard which leads from the carpark. If the exterior of the Club is impressive, internally it is fabulous. From the wood panelled lobby you look up to a lovely galleried landing constructed of local hardwood Totara, picked out in a pale blue which very cleverly softens the look. The Ladies Drawing Room leads off from the lobby. It is a sunny, north facing room, beautifully but still comfortably furnished and which seems to come into it's own for pre lunch drinks and for tea. The often very busy main dining room is a handsome, traditional room but bright, with 7 large arched windows which make the very best of even the pale winter sun. For more casual dining there is either the Buttery, a contemporarily decorated, recently refurbished room or the adjacent Orangery, a cheery, bright conservatory which has proved very popular from its outset. The Club prides itself on the standard of its food and it is indeed excellent, as is also, wholly unsurprisingly in New Zealand, the wine list. At the opposite end of the Club lies the Smoking Room (notional cigars however: New Zealand has banned smoking inside) with newspapers and magazines and where there is a seemingly permanent supply of coffee. Next to the Smoking Room, the Members bar, a cosy,

The Orangery

convivial and much used place where light lunches are also available on request. The walls here are hung with Club and Regimental plaques and with framed newspaper obituaries to the likes of former member Charles Upham, famous double VC and one of several hundred members who saw active service in one or other of the World Wars. And then, almost guiltily tucked away in the corner by the television are the original architect's plans drawn up in the 1960s for a new Clubhouse to replace the existing gem, plans which were defeated by only three votes. Phew. A close run thing. Moving on quickly from that minor horror, the grandest, most impressive room and perhaps somewhat surprisingly therefore, also the most comfortable is the Ante Room which looks out onto the east lawn. With big tall ceilings, an open fire at both ends of the room, horrifyingly expensive silk curtains, deep sofas and coffee tables littered with copies of Country Life it is every inch the classic country house drawing room. Much thought, money and taste has gone into the redecoration of this room and it works: it is magnetic and it is charming.

On the first floor is an excellent little business centre called the Tower Room complete with telephone, internet access, a small boardroom table and minibar. Also on the first floor with doors opening out onto the galleried landing are the 7 en suite, double rooms, all of which are spacious and comfortable and which have TV and minibars, some of which have views out over leafy Latimer Square.

In short, the Christchurch Club is an absolute jewel. If Christchurch itself is becoming a major holiday destination then this Club is the place to stay. Always a great Club, several of the members commented upon how it seems to have blossomed in recent years. Whatever the ideal recipe is, the Christchurch Club

Dining room (left); galleried landing (facing page)

has undoubtedly benefited from the active involvement of a very busy Women's Committee, a committee with which I think even GEF Kingscote, whose 1939 entry in the Suggestions book noting the inadmissibility of 'cats, banjoes or ladies to the premises' would have been impressed!

The Club lies 5 minutes' walk from Cathedral Square and less than 10 minutes from the Botanical Gardens and is 20 minutes by taxi from the airport. There is parking for 30 cars.

RECIPROCAL CLUBS

Canada
The Hamilton Club
Union Club of British Columbia
Rideau Club
The Vancouver Club

UK
The Caledonian Club
The Carlton Club
City University Club
The East India Club
The Farmers Club
The Hurlingham Club
The Lansdowne Club
The Naval and Military Club
The New Club Edinburgh
Oxford and Cambridge Club
Royal Air Force Club
The Royal Automobile Club
Royal Northern and University Club
The Royal Scots Club
The Travellers Club
The Western Club
Ulster Reform Club

Zimbabwe
Bulawayo Club

Kenya
Muthaiga Country Club
Nairobi Gymkhana Club

South Africa
Johannesburg Country Club
Victoria Country Club

Hong Kong
The Hong Kong Club

Thailand
The British Club

Singapore
The Tanglin Club

Australia
Athenaeum Club
The Commonwealth Club
The Melbourne Club
The Queensland Club
The Royal Automobile Club (Sydney)
United Service Club
Union Club Sydney
The Weld Club

New Zealand
Auckland Club
The Dunedin Club
Hawkes Bay Club
The Northern Club
The Wellington Club

The Dunedin Club

The hall

The Otago Club, as the Dunedin was then called, began life in 1858, barely 10 years after the first two settler ships, the John Wickliffe and the Phillip Laing, berthed in Dunedin harbour after the long voyage from Britain. Founded by runholders (farmers) who 'did not want to rough it in the old room with Tom, Dick and Harry and have old Gallie, the dirty blacksmith pop down on the chair next to you and ask you what you'll take', the Club occupied a series of temporary premises in town for the first 20 years of its life until it moved to Fernhill in 1874, by which time the Club had become the Old Dunedin Club. Fernhill as the Clubhouse was, and sometimes is still called, was designed by architect David Ross and was lived in by local whaler John

33 Melville Street
Dunedin
New Zealand

Tel: +64 3 477 0082
Fax: +64 3 477 0072

www.dunedinclub.co.nz
Email: gm@dunedinclub.co.nz

The club

Dining room

Jones and his wife Sarah until John's death in 1869, when the house was leased to the Provincial Government, becoming home to two successive Governors, Sir George Bowen and then Sir James Fergusson. Sarah sold the house to the Club in 1874 from which year it has been the Dunedin Club's very grand and comfortable home, being extended by Louis Boldini in later years in order to accommodate a card room and a billiard room.

The Clubs farming roots are evident in the very first entry in the suggestion book dating from February 4th, 1875, where 'pillar rails in the stables for fastening up a horse' are requested. Whilst the Club is still a home for out-of-town members, most

Food & Beverages
Dining Room
Guests' Breakfast Room
Bar

Sports facilities
Squash Court

Miscellaneous
Billiards Room
Reading Room
Business Centre

Accommodation
8 rooms: 5 singles, 2 doubles and 1 twin, all en suite, starting at NZ$75.

A Victorian lady immortalised in relief in the Reading Room, probably either Sarah Jones or the wife of Caption EHW Bellairs, the two previous owners of Fernhill before the Dunedin took possession.

The club by night

of the 410 members now are local Dunedin people. Dunedin was settled by the Scots, perhaps in part because both the topography and the weather are similar. The Clubhouse itself certainly reminds of Scotland: if you've been on a fishing trip to one of the great Scottish Rivers and have hired a lodge with a group of friends or stayed at one of the old fishing hotels, then you've seen Fernhill. To be so reminded of Scotland, a full half a world away, is uncanny. The town of Dunedin has suffered economically in recent years, losing out to Christchurch as a business destination of choice and the symptoms of this economic fact are reflected, not surprisingly, in the Club. The Club is not the richest, nor is it the most plush. Modernisation of the Clubs facilities has yet to happen in any meaningful way and will be a gradual process taking both time and money, although plans are underway. That said, Fernhill is a beautifully designed and well-built house, the proportions are glorious and there is a feeling of warm, comfortable space everywhere. The Dining Room is big and grand with tall ceilings and lovely views out over the lawns and the bar is both welcoming and busy. The rooms are comfortable and spacious and all are en suite.

There is a small and efficient business centre for those who cannot resist the call of the email.

The staff are an eclectic mix, some local, some from the far corners of the world, all of whom however appear to love the place and work hard to make it a success and to make guests feel welcome. Both the staff and the members are only too happy to describe and share their knowledge of the quite fantastic wildlife to be seen on the Peninsula, the abundant and (usually) free trout fishing and the stunning, wild and wooly countryside to be either walked over or viewed from the seat of a warm car. They will also tell you where to buy some of the increasingly good Otago Pinot Noirs. (Again from the Suggestions Book, 28th September 1971, a very prescient complaint from a member to the effect that the Club cellar did not do justice to the wine potential in New Zealand. One hopes he invested.)

Dunedin is remote: next stop east is Chile and next stop south is the ice. Indeed the harbour was the final mooring place of the Discovery before it took Captain Robert Scott and his crew to the Antarctic in 1901, the Club giving him and his Officers dinner the night before they left. (He was back

in 1910 aboard Terra Nova for his final and fateful voyage to the South Pole.) Being so far flung however, the most south easterly town in Australasia, Dunedin has yet to be firmly on the tourist trail—given the fishing, the countryside, the wine and the warmth of welcome, it will be, and the friendly and comfortable Dunedin Club is the perfect base from which to explore that trail.

The Club lies in the area known as Fernhill, no more than a ten-minute walk from the Octagon in the centre of town and is approximately 25 minutes by taxi from the Airport.

RECIPROCAL CLUBS

UK
The Army and Navy Club
Caledonian Club
The Carlton Club
The East India Club
The Hurlingham Club
The Lansdowne Club
The New Club Edinburgh
Royal Air Force Club
Royal Scots Club
The Travellers Club
The Western Club

South Africa
Cape Town Club
Durban Club
The Rand Club

Hong Kong
The Kowloon Cricket Club
Hong Kong Football Club
United Services Recreation Club

Thailand
The British Club

Singapore
The Tanglin Club

Australia
Athenaeum Club
Brisbane Polo Club
The Melbourne Club
Queensland Club
Tattersall's Club
Union Club (Sydney)
Union, University and Schools' Club of Sydney
The Weld Club

New Zealand
Auckland Club
The Christchurch Club
Hawkes Bay Club
The Northern Club
The Wellington Club

Hall entrance

Hawkes Bay Club

The clubhouse with adjoining garden

The pretty town of Napier lies on the east coast of the North Island of New Zealand. Popular with city dwellers as both a weekend escape and as a summer holidays destination, the town also attracts an increasingly large number of visitors from the wine trade drawn to the area by the growing reputation of the Hawkes Bay cabernet sauvignon and merlot grapes.

Napier is lovely: in the summer it is all ice cream, sunshine, blue skies and carefree days as families bucket and spade by the sea, or stroll along the neat and well-tended seafront. There is a sense of calm and a feeling of order here and the clock seems to tick that little more slowly, almost as if to allow people the time more fully to enjoy the balmy weather. Napier's other great draw

Marine Parade
PO Box 278
Napier
New Zealand

Tel: +64 6 835 7269
Fax: +64 6 835 0597

www.hawkesbayclub.co.nz
Email: hawkesbay.club@xtra.co.nz

Entrance foyer

Club stairways

is the almost uniformly period architecture, the town having been rebuilt largely in the Art Deco style following a violent earthquake in February 1931, which destroyed the majority of the town with what remained succumbing to a subsequent ferocious fire. So powerful had the earthquake been in fact that the mean height of the town above sea level was actually raised by several feet and in outlying suburbs, swamps drained and dykes emptied, and as if in pitifully small compensation for the loss of life and property, the town gained several thousand acres of new land. Very few buildings in the town survived these twin disasters: one which did however was the Hawkes Bay Club. Constructed of wood, with all that material's inherent flexibility, the Club 'rolled' with the earthquake's punches and remained standing. The flashpoint of the subsequent fire was several streets to the south, and, crucially downwind of, the Hawkes Bay Club and so was spared this beautiful building which stands almost unique today as a survivor of a pre-1931 Napier.

The Club began life in 1863 when the town of Napier was still barely 8 years old. After several temporary homes, in 1906

Food & Beverages
Dining Room
Members Bar
Verandah Bar (Room 5)

Accommodation
3 double rooms and 1 suite, each with TV beginning at NZ$85 per room.

Stairway looking down to the entrance foyer

Roll of Honour plaque

the Club members commissioned local architect WP Finch to design a purpose built Clubhouse for them at the northern end of Marine Parade and Finch's eye-catching creation has been the Club's home ever since. It is a beautiful, colonial style building with large, well-proportioned rooms, with walls throughout handsomely panelled of Rimu, a tough, local hardwood which mellows with age to a warm golden brown. On all sides are big, wide verandahs from where, on the first floor at least, you can gaze out to an extremely blue sea. The Club was originally founded by graziers who lived out in the country and who needed somewhere to stay when visiting town. There are still some rural members but it is now largely an urban Club drawing its members from the professions in Napier and from nearby Hastings.

The Hawkes Bay Club is a warm, unpretentious place with a friendly and relaxed feel about it. Whilst the Club does, unusually for New Zealand, still restrict full membership to men, the restriction is largely technical and women have full access to the Club's somewhat limited but nevertheless very good facilities. On both floors, all rooms lead off the extremely impressive, neo-baronial hall. Don't miss (it would be difficult to do so) the huge Marlin's head mounted on the wall on the ground floor which serves, almost as if by design, to wet the appetite of anybody in Napier for some deep sea fishing. The dining room is a grand but still comfortable room which is open for lunch 6 days per week and for dinner if booked. The food is simple and very good. There is also a reading room with local newspapers and a small library, a huge billiards room and a rather convivial Members Bar. On the first floor is (what the Club calls) Room 5: a bar and verandah with lovely sea views. The accommodation rooms though not fully modernised are clean and comfortable and they offer

Dining room

extremely good value. To the front of the Club, there is a delightful small terrace and garden where members often gather for early evening drinks. To the side and to the rear is parking for 12 cars. Noteworthy in this Club is the wine cellar, cellar in this context being more of a generic name for the business of storing wine wherever there's a space. Spend 20 minutes looking at the wines at the far end of the Members Bar—case after case of excellent Hawkes Bay reds laid down over the years by a committee with some foresight: the Club rightly prides itself on having one of the best wine lists in New Zealand.

The Hawkes Bay Club's location at the northern end of Napier's seafront is perfect for access to the beach (150 yards) and to the town centre (400 yards). Though certainly not glitzy, it is a warm, comfortable and spacious Club with a friendly membership and with helpful staff, and which offers the perfect base from which to explore this most unusual, Art Deco gem of a town, perched, as it is, on the very edge of the Southern Ocean.

RECIPROCAL CLUBS

Canada
The Halifax Club
The Union Club of British Columbia

UK
The Army and Navy Club
City University Club
The East India Club
The Farmers Club
The Lansdowne Club
The Naval and Military Club

South Africa
Cape Town Club
Durban Club

Australia
Athenaeum Club
The Commonwealth Club
Melbourne Savage Club

The Naval and Military Club (Melbourne)
The Naval, Military and Air Force Club
Queensland Club
United Service Club
The Union Club
The Weld Club

New Zealand
The Christchurch Club
The Dunedin Club
The Northern Club
The Wellington Club

The Marlin head mounted on the wall

The Northern Club

The Northern Club

The Northern Club is a triumph of sympathetic modernisation and is the perfect example of how the old and the new can be combined successfully and happily under the same roof. Its membership of 1,350, up 50 per cent in five years demonstrates the success of the changes made by a farsighted management and whether on business or on leave, The Northern Club very much fits the bill.

Originally a hotel, 19 Princes Street was redesigned in 1869 by architect Edward Rumsey as a Clubhouse for the 120 members of the newly formed Northern Club. Several of the

19 Princes Street
Auckland
New Zealand

Tel: +64 9 379 4755
Fax: +64 9 302 0909

www.northernclub.co.nz
Email: nicki@northernclub.co.nz

Hallway

Library

founding members were Officers of the 'Imperial' Army who, having no desire to return to Britain at the end of tour, handed in their papers and began a new life in Auckland. That the Club was initially run upon the same lines as the Army and Navy in London comes as no surprise therefore and there is still to this day, an indefinable but perceptible feel of a settled and comfortable Officers' mess about it. The building itself, more redolent of Edinburgh than London is a large, handsome, Virginia creeper covered Victorian townhouse, occupying a prime corner plot at the junction of Princes and Kitchener

Food & Beverages
Main Dining Room
Bankside Restaurant and Bar
Members Bar
Whisky Bar

Sports facilities
Gymnasium

Miscellaneous
Reading Room
Library
Billiards Room

Accommodation
8 double rooms, all en suite with minibar and television starting at NZ$130 per night.

Club entrance

Bankside Restaurant

Streets. Indisputably the dominant of the two Auckland Clubs, the membership these days is composed mainly of the civil professions with an average age which drops each year as new, younger members join. They are attracted by the modern 'half' of the Club, part of which is the minimalist and chic Bankside restaurant and bar with its own verandah and part of which is a small but very well-equipped gymnasium, both of which lie to the rear of the Club. Bankside is the Club's answer to the desire of younger professionals to have dinner in a more contemporary environment and has proved popular, drawing many for drinks in the evening to its ultra modern, uplit bar and also to the restaurant which serves delicious food and which has a well chosen list of top New Zealand wines. The combination of these two new builds, collocated in the same area of the Club attracts many younger members who want a light lunch after some exercise before heading back to the office and has proved a great success.

The more traditional side of the Club, and no less attractive for being so, is similar in feel to a Scottish lodge with tall ceilings, panelled walls and a great feeling of space. On the ground floor leading off a grand hall hung with antlers and with monster

Members Bar

trout is the Members' Bar, recently refurbished, traditional and convivial. Opposite lies the Whisky Bar complete with 48 different Scottish single malts. Further along is a Reading Room with daily newspapers which also doubles as a business centre with computer and internet access and then at the end of the hall, the main dining room, an impressive, bright, nicely old-fashioned place, which has a menu and a wine list of equal quality to that in Bankside, and whose walls are hung with some valuable portraits of Royalty painted by Sir William Beechey and Sir William Dargey.

On the first floor is a quiet, peaceful little library, something of a haven for those who need to work or write letters and which houses a tremendous collection of books on New Zealand donated by former member Dr George Fenwick. The Club has 8 double rooms, all en suite, some of which have been refurbished but all of which are more than comfortable and serviceable. The Club is open for accommodation and for breakfast 7 days per week, but irritatingly and a little surprisingly, closes for dinner on the weekends. That minor hiccup apart, The Northern Club is an absolutely first rate Club, well run, smart and comfortable which will get only better as a program of further refurbishments gathers pace. The Club lies only 2 blocks from the centre of town and is 25 minutes by taxi from the Airport.

Main dining room

RECIPROCAL CLUBS

Canada
The Ontario Club
Rideau Club
The Union Club of British Columbia
The University Club of Montreal
The Vancouver Club

UK
Bath and Country Club
Caledonian Club
The Carlton Club
The East India Club
The Hurlingham Club
The Lansdowne Club
Leander Club
The Naval and Military Club
The Naval Club
The New Club Edinburgh
Oriental Club
The Royal Automobile Club
The Travellers Club
Ulster Reform Club
The University Women's Club
The Western Club

South Africa
Cape Town Club
Johannesburg Country Club
Victoria Country Club

Hong Kong
Foreign Correspondents' Club
The Hong Kong Club

Thailand
The British Club

Singapore
The Tanglin Club
Singapore Cricket Club

Australia
Athenaeum Club
The Brisbane Club
The Commonwealth Club
The Melbourne Club
Queensland Club
The Royal Automobile Club
Union Club (Sydney)
The Weld Club

New Zealand
Auckland Club
The Christchurch Club
The Dunedin Club
Hawkes Bay Club
The Wellington Club

The Wellington Club

The ante room

The Wellington Club is one of New Zealand's oldest and indeed proudest institutions. Founded in 1841 by early Wellington settlers it has counted most of the great and the good of New Zealand society amongst it's members and has gained for itself a rather special role in that country's capital city as an almost 'must join' for foreign diplomats. Despite its old lineage the Club has a new, urban feel about it, a feel which is very much in touch with modern Wellington and the clever retention of the old standards and manners whilst at the same time embracing the social and business realities of modern city life has ensured both a very wide age range across the 1,330 membership and also the Club's continuing success.

Level 4
88 The Terrace
Wellington
New Zealand

Tel: +64 4 472 0348
Fax: +64 4 472 2475

www.wellingtonclub.co.nz
Email: info@wellingtonclub.co.nz

*6th floor looking towards the Business
Centre and Casual Dining Room*

5th floor galleried hall

The Club occupies the top three floors of a seven-storey building which it owns outright and which lies on The Terrace, one of the smartest addresses in Wellington on the edge of the CBD. The site has been the Club's home since 1877 when it moved into a lovely, Thomas Turnbull-designed neo-colonial house which tragically had to give way to a motorway in 1971. The Club then 'squatted' in an interim Clubhouse known irreverently as the Noddy House for 12 years until the current building by Sir Miles Warren was completed, being formally opened by the Duke of Edinburgh in 1990 (as half of the old was knocked down, half of the new was built thus ensuring continuous service throughout the entire operation—an engineering and organisational masterpiece). The

Food & Beverages
Main Dining Room
Casual Dining Room and Bar
Members' Bar
Ante room: drinks

Sports facilities
Gymnasium
Squash Court

Accommodation
8 double and 2 twin rooms, each with TV, mini bar, aircon and internet access beginning at NZ$187 per night.

Miscellaneous
Business Centre
Billiards Room
Laundry Service

Billards room

The Quadrant Room; dining room; reading room (left to right)

new building, modern obviously, is nevertheless elegant and the fine, crescent shaped frontage is inspired by the crescent-shaped canopy of the Pohutukawa tree which stands in front of the Club, a much loved tree planted by Club President and King's Council Martin Chapman in 1895.

Access to the 4th floor reception is via a lift in the main lobby. Here are the offices and function rooms and also the Reading Room and Library which holds the daily newspapers. The heart of the Club is really the 5th floor where are to be found the lovely ante room in the centre of the crescent and also the Members' Bar. Here also is the Main Dining Room which is smart and where they pride themselves on a hard won reputation for very good food. Separate tables can be reserved here for business or for private lunches: if dining alone, the Club works on the Mess principal where you sit next to the last person on the refectory tables: all very civilised. On the 6th floor is a brand new Gymnasium, a Business Centre, a more casual Dining Room cum Bar for light lunches and also the Quadrant Room where breakfast is served to guests. The 10 accommodation rooms are excellent and occupancy rates are high. The Club is 20 minutes by taxi from the Airport and is but a few minutes' walk from the centre of town. There is private, secure underground parking for 38 cars.

A good, well run and efficient Club which very much meets the demands of modern city life: for the reciprocating visitor to Wellington, the fuss-free efficiency, extensive facilities and ideal location of the Club make it pretty much ideal.

RECIPROCAL CLUBS

Canada
The Union Club of British Columbia
The Vancouver Club

UK
The Army and Navy Club
Athenaeum Club
Caledonian Club
The Carlton Club
The Cavalry and Guards Club
The East India Club
The Hurlingham Club
Leander Club
The Naval and Military Club
The Naval Club
The New Club Edinburgh
Oxford and Cambridge Club
The Royal Automobile Club
Royal Northern and University Club
The Travellers Club

Kenya
The Nairobi Club

South Africa
The Cape Town Club
The Durban Club

Hong Kong
The Hong Kong Club
United Services Recreation Club

Australia
The Queensland Club
The Commonwealth Club
Athenaeum Club (Melbourne)
The Melbourne Club
The Naval and Military Club (Melbourne)
The Weld Club Perth
The Union Club Sydney
The Royal Automobile Club (Sydney)

New Zealand
The Auckland Club
The Christchurch Club
The Dunedin Club
The Hawkes Bay Club
The Northern Club

The club (top three floors) from the terrace

Postscript

*I*t is with enormous pleasure that Mullis Partners took the opportunity of being associated with Stephen Simmons' wonderful book. I first heard of Stephen's plan to write the book on returning from Melbourne. A colleague of mine and I had to travel at the last minute to Melbourne and as the Commonwealth Games were on, we found ourselves in the rather undesirable position of hotels being full or so over-priced as to cause us to rethink the trip. My secretary cleverly remembered that a club I belong to in Bangkok had reciprocity with a Melbourne club. So we were in luck and found ourselves with excellent rooms at a considerably lower cost than any hotel that I had stayed at in Melbourne before.

Stephen's book is a gem. In writing it, Stephen has done great service to the clubs mentioned and to travellers worldwide. I am sure that those of you who take the opportunity of visiting these clubs will find that Robert Louis Stevenson's famous saying perhaps should have added to it the words in italics, 'to travel hopefully is a better thing than to arrive—*but arriving is pure joy*'.

ROBERT MULLIS
Bangkok

Acknowledgement

$\mathcal{T}$his book would not have been possible without the generous assistance and goodwill of many people. First and foremost, I am grateful to the Secretaries and General Managers of all the Clubs which I visited during the year-long research for this book. They all took a bit of a leap in the dark by permitting me, an unknown quantity, to write about their Clubs and I hope I have done them justice. Secondly, I would have been stumped on many an occasion without the help of Bangkok-based photojournalist and good friend, Dominic Faulder. He was a model of patience and a mine of good advice, and without his assistance, writing this book would have been a much more difficult task. Also Bangkok-based, Investment Banker and friend Robert Mullis has shown great faith in the idea behind the book by generously shouldering some costs for which I profoundly thank him. Of course, no book can thrive without a good publisher and I am grateful to Editions Didier Millet for their flair and for their drive. They are the 'blue chips' of the Asian publishing world and I am lucky that they took this book under their wing.

I also thank Nick Shryane who managed to find the time to write the foreword from the busy and hallowed depths of the Bursary at Harrow School in London.

By accompanying me on my travels, my wife Caroline has turned what might have been a mere pleasure into an absolute delight, as has always been the case, happily for me, throughout her 25 years 'following the drum'.

Lastly, I am grateful to my parents who took us all to live in the New Territories of Hong Kong in 1966 and in so doing, gave me the 'bug' for the East.

Photo Credits

The author and publisher would like to thank the following for permission to reproduce the photographs: (Editions Didier Millet) Publisher's collection: *2-3, 21, 66, 68, 86*; Foreign Correspondents' Club Hong Kong: *24, 26-28*; The Helena May Club: *1, 15, 24, 29-31*; The Naval and Military Club: *110-113*; Stew Robertson: *144-145;* Sin Kam Cheong: *84-85;* Tanglin Club: *94, 96*; Picture Courtesy of Timothy Auger: *91*

Reciprocal Club Listing

CANADA
Albany Club, The
Edmonton Petroleum Club
Glencoe Club, The
Halifax Club, The
Hamilton Club
Hollyburn Country Club
Montefiore Club (Montreal)
Mount Royal Club (Montreal), The
Mount Stephen Club
National Club (Ontario)
National Club, The
National Liberal Club (Toronto), The
Ontario Club, The
Rideau Club
Rideau Tennis Club (Ontario)
Royal Canadian Military Institute, The
Royal Canadian Yacht Club
Royal Nova Scotia Yacht Squadron
Royal Vancouver Yacht Club
Royal Victoria Yacht Club
St. James's Club (Montreal)
Union Club of British Columbia, The
University Club of Toronto, The
Vancouver Club, The
Vancouver Lawn Tennis &
Badminton Club

UK
Army and Navy Club, The
Athenaeum Club
Ballyholme Yacht Club
Bath and Country Club
Bucks Club
Caledonian Club
Carlton Club, The
Cavalry and Guards Club, The
City University Club
Commonwealth Club, The
East India Club, The
Farmers Club, The
Hurlingham Club, The
Lansdowne Club, The
Leander Club
London Press Club
National Liberal Club, The
Naval and Military Club, The
Naval Club, The
New Cavendish Club, The
New Club Edinburgh, The
New Club, Cheltenham
New Club, The
Norfolk Club, The
Nottingham & Nottinghamshire, The
Nottingham Club, The
Oriental Club
Oxford and Cambridge Club
Phyllis Court Club
Reform Club, The
Royal Air Force Club
Royal Air Force Yacht Club
Royal Automobile Club, The
Royal Channel Islands Yacht Club
Royal Corinthian Yacht Club
Royal Cornwall Yacht Club
Royal Dart Yacht Club
Royal Naval Club and Royal Albert
Yacht Club
Royal Northern and University Club
Royal Over-Seas League
Royal Scots Club
Royal Southern Yacht Club
Royal Thames Yacht Club
St. James's Club
St. James's Club (London)
St. James's Club (Manchester)
Travellers Club, The
Ulster Reform Club
United Oxford & Cambridge University Club
United Service Club
University Women's Club, The
Victoria Club
Western Club, The
Wig & Pen Club

THE NETHERLANDS
Royal Netherlands Yacht Club

SEYCHELLES
Seychelles Yacht Club

ZIMBABWE
Bulawayo Club
Harare Club

KENYA

Mombasa Club, The
Muthaiga Country Club
Nairobi Gymkhana Club

SOUTH AFRICA

Cape Town Club
Johannesburg Country Club
Durban Club
Durban Country Club
Gordon's Bay Yacht Club
Inanda Club
Johannesburg Country Club
Kimberley Club, The
Rand Club, The
Royal Cape Yacht Club
Victoria Country Club

HONG KONG

Aberdeen Boat Club
Foreign Correspondents' Club
Hong Kong Club, The
Hong Kong Cricket Club
Hong Kong Football Club
Hong Kong Golf Club
Kowloon Cricket Club, The
Ladies' Recreation Club
Royal Hong Kong Yacht Club
United Services Recreation Club

THAILAND

British Club, The
Capitol Club, The
Foreign Correspondents' Club
Royal Bangkok Sports Club, The
Royal Varuna Yacht Club

MALAYSIA

Penang Club
Penang Sports Club
Penang Swimming Club
Raintree Club
Royal Commonwealth Society, The
Royal Ipoh Club
Royal Lake Club
Royal Port Dickson Yacht Club
Royal Selangor Club

SINGAPORE

Changi Sailing Club
Foreign Correspondents' Club
Hollandse Club
Singapore Cricket Club
Singapore Polo Club
Tanglin Club, The

AUSTRALIA

Athenaeum Club
Australian Club, The
Brisbane Club, The

Brisbane Polo Club
Canberra Club, The
City Tattersalls Club
Club of Sydney
Commonwealth Club, The
Geelong Club, The
Huntingdon Club
Kelvin Club, The
Lyceum Club (Melbourne)
Melbourne Club, The
Melbourne Savage Club
Middle Harbour Yacht Club
National Press Club
Naval and Military Club (Melbourne), The
Naval, Military and Air Force Club, The
North Queensland Club
Queensland Club
Queensland Cricketers' Club
Royal Automobile Club (Melbourne), The
Royal Automobile Club (Sydney), The
Royal Automobile Club, The
Royal Brighton Yacht Club
Royal Exchange
Royal Geelong Yacht Club
Royal Melbourne Yacht Squadron
Royal Perth Golf Club
Royal Perth Yacht Club
Royal South Yarra Lawn Tennis Club
Royal Sydney Yacht Squadron
Sandringham Club, The
Southport Yacht Club
Tattersall's Club
Tattersall's Club (Brisbane)
Tattersall's Club (Sydney)
Union Club (Sydney)
Union, University and Schools' Club of Sydney
United Service Club
Victorian Club
Weld Club, The
Western Australian Club, The

NEW ZEALAND

Auckland Club
Bucklands Beach Yacht Club
Canterbury Club, The
Christchurch Club, The
Dunedin Club, The
Hamilton Club, The
Hawkes Bay Club
National Press Club
Northern Club, The
Royal New Zealand Yacht Club
Royal Port Nicholson Yacht Club
Wellington Club, The

*Hawkes Bay Club (pages 160–161); The Helena
May Club (page 162); The Dunedin Club (page
164); The Helena May Club (page 166)*